A SENSE OF COLOUR

Series 7™ Chair (3107) by Arne Jacobsen in Evergreen
with Brown Bronze base and front upholstery in Sunniva 3.

Explore more at **fritzhansen.com**

Stay where the world can't find you.

Cottages and small hotels in the wild Scottish Highlands

TF Design
Modern Designs in Resin

tf.design

tf

Loopy Vase

HOUSE OF
FINN JUHL

CHIEFTAIN CHAIR | 1949 | FINNJUHL.COM

HFJ

KINFOLK

MAGAZINE

—

EDITOR IN CHIEF	John Clifford Burns
EDITOR	Harriet Fitch Little
ART DIRECTOR	Christian Møller Andersen
DESIGN DIRECTOR	Alex Hunting
COPY EDITOR	Rachel Holzman
FACT CHECKER	Fedora Abu

STUDIO

—

ADVERTISING, SALES & DISTRIBUTION DIRECTOR	Edward Mannering
STUDIO & PROJECT MANAGER	Susanne Buch Petersen
DESIGNER & ART DIRECTOR	Staffan Sundström
DIGITAL MANAGER	Cecilie Jegsen

—

CROSSWORD	Mark Halpin
PUBLICATION DESIGN	Alex Hunting Studio
COVER PHOTOGRAPHS	Salva López

The views expressed in *Kinfolk* magazine are those of the respective contributors and are not necessarily shared by the company or its staff. *Kinfolk* (ISSN 2596-6154) is published quarterly by Ouur ApS, Amagertorv 14B, 2, 1160 Copenhagen, Denmark. Printed by Park Communications Ltd in London, United Kingdom. Color reproduction by Park Communications Ltd in London, United Kingdom. All rights reserved. No part of this publication may be reproduced, distributed or transmitted in any form or by any means, including photocopying or other electronic or mechanical methods, without prior written permission of the editor in chief, except in the case of brief quotations embodied in critical reviews and certain other noncommercial uses permitted by copyright law. The US annual subscription price is $87 USD. Airfreight and mailing in the USA by WN Shipping USA, 156-15, 146th Avenue, 2nd Floor, Jamaica, NY 11434, USA. Application to mail at periodicals postage prices is pending at Jamaica NY 11431. US Postmaster: Send address changes to Kinfolk, WN Shipping USA, 156-15, 146th Avenue, 2nd Floor, Jamaica, NY 11434, USA. Subscription records are maintained at Ouur ApS, Amagertorv 14B, 2, 1160 Copenhagen, Denmark. SUBSCRIBE: *Kinfolk* is published four times a year. To subscribe, visit kinfolk.com/subscribe or email us at info@kinfolk.com. CONTACT US: If you have questions or comments, please write to us at info@kinfolk.com. For advertising and partnership inquiries, get in touch at advertising@kinfolk.com.

WORDS

—

Precious Adesina
Aida Alami
Allyssia Alleyne
Alex Anderson
Poppy Beale-Collins
Nana Biamah-Ofosu
Katie Calautti
James Clasper
Stephanie d'Arc Taylor
Michelle Del Rey
Daphnée Denis
Aindrea Emelife
Layli Foroudi
Bella Gladman
Harry Harris
Anissa Helou
Robert Ito
Sabina Llewellyn-Davies
Nathan Ma
Sarah Manavis
Lina Mounzer
Brian Ng
Okechukwu Nzelu
Hettie O'Brien
John Ovans
Debika Ray
Laura Rysman
Charles Shafaieh
Baya Simons
Sarah Souli
George Upton

STYLING, SET DESIGN, HAIR & MAKEUP

—

Anastasiia Babii
Juan Camilo Rodríguez
Gill Linton
Jean-Charles Perrier
Déborah Sadoun
Stephanie Stamatis

ARTWORK & PHOTOGRAPHY

—

Sébastien Baert
Lauren Bamford
Martina Bjorn
Luc Braquet
Yoann Cimier
Sadie Culberson
Bea De Giacomo
Marina Denisova
Daniel Farò
Justin French
Stephanie Gonot
François Halard
Christian Heikoop
Cecilie Jegsen
Nicola Kloosterman
Chris Kontos
Romain Laprade
Laurence Leenaert
Salva López
Karima Maruan
Andy Massaccesi
Rick McGinnis
Arch McLeish
Christian Møller Andersen
Tahmineh Monzavi
Ezra Patchett
Noé Sendas
Mirka Laura Severa
Laila Sieber
Jules Slutsky
Bachar Srour
Victor Stonem
Armin Tehrani
Emma Trim
Alex Wolfe

PUBLISHER

—

Chul-Joon Park

COMING SOON
The new book from *Kinfolk*

The latest book from the team behind *Kinfolk* magazine celebrates slow travel and the idea that an attitude of discovery is more meaningful than any particular action or itinerary. Featuring over 25 beautiful destinations across six continents, *Kinfolk Travel* offers an easy, mindful approach to exploring the world at your own pace, whether you're five or five thousand miles from home.

WELCOME
Beside the Seaside

The Mediterranean exists as a vacation preset in many people's holiday imaginings: not simply a sea, but a near mythological fantasy.

The reality is that there are relatively few places where the Mediterranean, a region that consists of 22 countries extending over 30,000 miles of coastline, resembles the idyll of a picture postcard—and the few spots that do are already very busy.

In this issue of *Kinfolk*, we venture beyond the rivieras to seek out quieter stretches of the land that hugs the sea. Over 60 pages, the Mediterranean Issue will transport you from Tuscany to Tunis, Arles to Athens, and Mallorca to Morocco (and some less alliterative, but equally compelling, destinations), highlighting the creativity, warmth and hospitality that endures around the region long after the last flight departs at the end of the summer season.

In Beirut, we meet Victor Chebli, the lighthouse keeper who has weathered storms, war and three kidnappings in his determination to keep a watchful eye over his stretch of the sea. On a remote ranch in Tuscany, writer Laura Rysman meets the *butteri*—the last Italian cowboys—while in Tangier, we visit a beloved art house cinema that was bootstrapped by artist Yto Barrada and has since blossomed as the heart and soul of the city's creative scene. Our feature fashion shoot brings to life a sleepy day on the Catalonian coast, and, for those who need to be sated with a slice of sunshine as soon as possible, chef Anissa Helou has shared recipes for a three-course Moroccan meal.

While we have avoided certain clichés in putting together this issue, the beautiful images and stories gathered here certainly fuel their own fantasy of Mediterranean living. It is all of our responsibilities to also keep our eyes open to the realities of the world we write about: In the Mediterranean section, we interview Olivia Spili, a first responder for Sea-Watch, an NGO which provides emergency relief to those attempting the desperately dangerous sea crossing from North Africa to Southern Europe in search of safety.

The rest of the stories in this issue sail an offbeat course to some interesting destinations elsewhere in the world: Northern Ireland, to meet the family behind the furniture brand Orior; the Dominican Republic, to see inside the home of interior designer Patricia Reid Baquero; and Berlin, to meet the extraordinary architect Diébédo Francis Kéré. To cap it all off, we interview a woman who can't be contained by geography, or career, or convention: the legendary Michèle Lamy.

WORDS
JOHN CLIFFORD BURNS
HARRIET FITCH LITTLE

marset

Taking care of light

STARTERS
Laundry, spaghetti & virtual sundries.

FEATURES
Paris to Berlin... via the Caribbean.

"I don't waste time talking about sustainability as fashion." (Diébédo Francis Kéré – P. 93)

Photograph: Salva López

"Tradition keeps this work alive... You have to love it as a way of life."   (Stefano Pavin – P. 119)

THE MEDITERRANEAN
The other side of the seaside.

DIRECTORY
Creative stubs and a crossword.

Photograph: Andy Massaccesi

Born in 1949. Thousands of new combinations yet to be discovered.

string®

String Shelving System combined by interior designer Lo Bjurulf. Discovered in 2021.

19 — 48

20

WE'LL ALWAYS HAVE PARIS
The clichéd capital of comparison.

There is a Paris, it seems, in every region. You can find a "Paris of the East" in Shanghai, Bucharest, Kabul or Pondicherry, and a "Paris of the North" in Copenhagen, Warsaw and Riga. Across the Atlantic, Paris has been found in Havana ("Paris of the Caribbean"), Detroit ("Paris of the Midwest"), Kansas City ("Paris of the Plains") and Montreal ("Paris of the New World"). In 1943, when trying to entice Franklin D. Roosevelt to accompany him to Marrakech following a Casablanca summit, Winston Churchill famously termed the city the "Paris of the Sahara."[1]

These comparisons are about more than cafés, liberal values, boulevards and art deco apartments—in many instances brought in under the force of colonial rule. In fact, the literal similarities are often beside the point. To evoke Paris is to align a place with one of the most revered, most visited and most iconic cities on the planet. In the West, it's to make the unknown or untested familiar and alluring—a place worth caring about.

While the origin of the turn of phrase is indeterminable, Paris' image as a city of Western fascination is long established. During the 17th and 18th centuries, it was a rite of passage for men of the upper classes to stop by the French capital on their Grand Tour of Europe. By the 19th century, when industrialization made international travel cheaper and easier, Paris had come to epitomize what a good Western city should be: full of grand monuments to admire, people to watch, wide streets to roam and elegant shops to peruse.

"The metropolis had become, beyond all question, the most beautiful city in the world," the American historian John Stevens Cabot Abbott wrote in 1873, to contextualize the brief reign of Napoleon III from 1852 to 1870. "The English complained that the attractions of Paris were such, that American travellers, crossing the ocean by thousands, made London but a stepping-stone to the French metropolis."

Throughout the 20th century, comparisons to Paris became more common, the stuff of snappy headlines and travel guides seeking to raise a lesser-known location's social currency by association. But as a sloganeering cliché, the "Paris of X" setup is inherently facile and small-minded. Through this Eurocentric lens, value is only found in that which conforms to an image of Western civility and recognized power.

But more than anything, this phrasing seems dated, a relic of a time when horizons felt small and the world unknowable. As globalization and mass media have homogenized culture, difference presents a greater draw.

Anyone travelling to Marrakech in search of the Paris of the Sahara will likely find themselves disappointed. But they may also find themselves entranced by something decidedly foreign—just as Churchill was. "Here in these spacious palm groves rising from the desert the traveller can be sure of perennial sunshine, of every comfort and diversion, and can contemplate with ceaseless satisfaction the stately and snow-clad panorama of the Atlas Mountains," he wrote in a 1936 article for *The Daily Mail* of the city that "captivated" him.

For those who can't look beyond the clichés, we'll always have Paris proper.

WORDS
ALLYSSIA ALLEYNE
PHOTO
ARMIN TEHRANI /
VÆRNIS STUDIO

(1) Churchill was so enamored with Morocco that he painted no less than 40 artworks during his visits. One, *Tower of the Koutoubia Mosque*, which he painted following the Casablanca Conference in 1943, eventually ended up in the hands of Angelina Jolie, who sold it at auction in March 2021 for $9.9 million.

ADOBE ACROBATS
Made for the moon, built in Iran.

WORDS
GEORGE UPTON
PHOTO
TAHMINEH MONZAVI

Colorful organic forms have begun to appear on the sparsely populated western shore of Hormuz Island in Iran, rising up out of the island's distinctive red sand. The initiative of Tehran-based ZAV Architects, the clusters of domed structures—vacation homes, restaurants, cafés and shops—are part of an ongoing project to empower the island's community while encouraging tourism and investment.

Central to the scheme is superadobe, an innovative building technique that uses local resources and that can be carried out by unskilled workers. Pioneered by the late Iranian architect Nader Khalili in the 1980s, superadobe was developed in response to a call from NASA for proposals for settlements that could be built on the moon. Khalili came up with the idea of filling polypropylene sacks with moon dust, which could be stacked in coils to create walls and domed ceilings. The technique has since

been employed everywhere from Nepal to refugee camps in Jordan, using whatever is available locally in the place of moon dust. Plastered and made watertight, the structures have survived earthquakes and hurricanes.

In Hormuz, the superadobe project promises not only to generate new sources of income, it has also given the people there a central role in creating a sustainable future for the island. Though Hormuz shares its name with the strait through which around a quarter of the world's oil passes—and which has often been a flashpoint between Iran and the West—the small volcanic island has historically been cut off and economically deprived. Now, using sand dredged from the Hormuz dock and the efforts of local people, the project has become a striking and vibrant new archetype for community-led architecture.

ISABEL SANDOVAL

WORDS
NATHAN MA
PHOTO
SADIE CULBERSON

On the limits of autobiography.

Filmmaker Isabel Sandoval works delicately, crafting lingering portraits of the love shared between her protagonists: a trans woman caring for a young boy in a small town, or an interracial couple eliding miscegenation laws during the Great Depression. Drawing from Almodóvar, Wong Kar-wai, Fassbinder and Bergman, Sandoval broke through in 2019 with *Lingua Franca*, a sensual, moving feature she wrote, directed and starred in. And she won a €10,000 prize at this year's Berlinale to produce her next film, *Tropical Gothic*. Having recently moved from New York to North Carolina, Sandoval is adjusting to a slower pace of life when we speak.

NATHAN MA: Many of your films center on the labor of caregiving. Why is that?

ISABEL SANDOVAL: I think it's both cultural, as a Filipina filmmaker, and the fact that those are the kinds of characters I gravitate toward. I'm just psychoanalyzing myself, but it's the kind of character that I yearn to be in real life: part of a family, caring for and looking after someone else. I was raised by my mom, who was a single parent, and I'm an only child. It's that yearning for belonging and community, and the symbiotic relationship between someone who gives care and love, and the person receiving it.

NM: When it comes to marginalized writers, artists and filmmakers, people often read authorship as autobiography. What do these readings miss?

IS: My work is deeply personal, but not autobiographical. In *Lingua Franca*, for instance, both the main character and I are Filipina trans women living in New York, but ultimately the similarities end there. It's still deeply personal in the sense that the characters I write are my creation, and there is a psychological and emotional truth and resonance in my life that I project onto these characters.

NM: What truths do you worry the audience might overlook when watching *Lingua Franca*?

IS: To say that the film's about an undocumented Filipina trans woman is reductive: Olivia, the main character, has ambition, and she is more than the sum of her different intersectional identities, and that's what I strive to do. The course of the film forces the audience to grapple with and understand this character as more than a trans woman looking for love, or an undocumented immigrant looking for papers.

NM: Your films are often set at the intersection of the personal and the political, whether that's Brooklyn under Trump, or the Philippines under Marcos. How do you navigate that intersection?

IS: My films tend to be set [amid] particular historic and cataclysmic events that are pivotal moments. They're not objective or impartial, because they're very much seen from the point of view of the protagonist. *Apparition*, my second feature, is not a third-person objective piece on life under martial law. It's about the unraveling that the characters experience because of a traumatic incident that happens halfway through the film. I take the same approach with my upcoming film *Tropical Gothic*, which is set in the Philippines in the 16th century, very early on during the Spanish regime. My primary concern is psychological realism, because to me, making art is essentially a gesture of empathetic imagination.

DIRTY WORK
A taxonomy of muck.

"What would happen if suddenly, magically, men could menstruate and women could not?" With this question posed at the outset of her famous essay *If Men Could Menstruate*, Gloria Steinem imagined a society in which men would make periods an "enviable, worthy, masculine event." Rather than being seen as an embarrassment or something to hide, "that time of the month" would become a sign of courage in patriarchal societies, she argued. Scientists would prioritize researching the origin of stomach cramps over heart attacks, from which menstruating men would be hormonally protected. All in all, what many societies have traditionally deemed dirty would instantly become an element of pride.

Though fictional, Steinem's essay allows readers to take in one simple truth: Dirt, and indeed all things perceived as unpleasant, is in the eye of the beholder. What some groups of people consider pure, others will find unclean, as theorized by British anthropologist Mary Douglas. Dirt, she wrote, is simply matter out of place. Blood inside one's body is normal but finding it anywhere else can prompt squeamishness. A foot may be clean, but putting one's feet on the dining table is certainly frowned upon. A fingernail isn't particularly dirty when it's on a hand, but that changes as soon as said nail ends up on the floor.

Dirt is relative, Douglas points out, because what we consider impure is that which breaks our social order, and different peoples have different sets of rules. In a household, things are dirty when they don't belong where they are. In a larger social context, however, the implications are far-reaching: Social systems are built around what people consider pure or polluted. Hygiene guidelines, insofar as they are used to determine what is pure, become a way to organize society and control human behavior. Whether religious or not, alcohol bans, rules about women's premarital virginity, the taboo surrounding periods, or even foods banned from consumption, all contribute to the way people are policed into acting. Needless to say, women and marginalized groups have historically gotten the short end of the stick. Indeed, as Douglas pointed out, the construct of purity is the enemy of change.

WORDS
DAPHNÉE DENIS
PHOTO
MARINA DENISOVA

A LOAD OF CRAP
The sanctity of cheap stuff.

WORDS
KATIE CALAUTTI
PHOTO
ARCH MCLEISH

Filling personal spaces with purely decorative, cheaply made trinkets—or tchotchkes, knickknacks, bric-a-brac, junk—is as American as apple pie. "Over time, Americans have decided—as individuals, as members of groups, and as a society—to embrace not just materialism itself but materials with a certain shoddy complexion," writes author Wendy A. Woloson in her book *Crap: A History of Cheap Stuff in America*.

The country's proud heritage of excess began during the consumer revolution of the 1700s, when artisans created inexpensive replicas of in-demand exotic goods; faux-wood finishes and paste gems imbued a sense of luxury. Soon, traveling salesmen were hawking cheap goods to people on the lower rungs of the social strata. All of those unnecessary baubles became "conduits through which Americans could envision better lives," Woloson writes. Items easily discarded and replaced also lowered the stakes of ownership—people no longer had to meticulously care for a precious few costly goods over a long period of time.

The burgeoning railroads and canals of the 19th century transported inexpensive goods to further reaches of the country, and variety stores sprang up. Americans saw themselves as consumers, taking pride in their ability to buy and display. Pop Momand's 1913 comic strip, "Keeping Up with the Joneses," was based on this socioeconomic phenomenon, and the title remains a popular idiom for embracing materialism.

Americans also championed being at the forefront of innovation and efficiency—cheap gadgets supplemented clunky, costly tools, not just halving the time of shucking corn or washing clothes, but transforming drudgery into entertainment. The combined need for functionality and low-risk purchasing has persisted, as evidenced by the popularity of QVC, As Seen On TV stores and SkyMall catalogs. Amazon updates its most popular gadgets page hourly.

The true worth of novelty or collectors' items, gift shop souvenirs or promotional goods lies in the eyes of its owner. "What constitutes crap is highly personal and historically contextual," Woloson writes.[1] However their material cost is defined, Americans' abundant, cheap possessions have become a vital component of identity—and therefore a meaningful clue to who we are.

(1) Cheap items are often referred to using a synonym for bodily waste, Woloson writes, because "crappy things are, in various ways, excrescences — quickly used up and happily, even proudly, disposed of."

MIXED EMOJI

WORDS
OKECHUKWU NZELU
PHOTO
BEA DE GIACOMO

Is a picture worth a thousand words?

Emoji are an established part of digital life. Still, few of us think about them in terms of linguistics. "As a system of communication, they leave English, the world's global language, in the dust," says Dr. Vyvyan Evans, language expert and digital communication technologist. Evans, who wrote *The Emoji Code* in 2017, insists that there is much to learn from eggplant and "crying-laughing" emoji about the way humans communicate.

OKECHUKWU NZELU: Is emoji a language?

VYVYAN EVANS: No. A language functions meaningfully in two directions. The first is a "words-to-world" fit. That means the words represent ideas in the world, either concrete (a physical thing, like a cat) or abstract (like feminism). And the second is a "word-to-word" fit: basically, a grammar. Emoji only does one part of the words-to-world fit: It is only able to signify concrete meanings. An emoji is good at representing a cat; it's less good at symbolizing feminism. And emoji cannot be used in a word-to-word direction—it can't be used as a grammatical system. So it falls foul, from that perspective, of being a language. It's what I call a code.

ON: I gather there are examples of the use of emoji being scrutinized in court. How do linguistics operate in that context?

VE: In 2015, I was contacted by *The Guardian* because there was a big story which related to a 17-year-old from New York, who had posted [on social media] an emoji of a police officer, and three handgun emoji pointing at the officer. This led to a report by the New York Police Department to the district attorney, who issued an arrest warrant. The 17-year-old was then arraigned before a grand jury, on the basis of anti-terrorist statutes introduced following 9/11. But there was no indictment, and this got me thinking about the similarities and differences between emoji and language. The jury effectively decided that the defendant intended to convey, through emoji's symbolic function, that guns should be aimed at police—but he didn't mean to incite violence against them through the use of emoji's performative function.

ON: Does our use of emoji mirror other linguistic principles?

VE: One example is from Lizzo, the American rapper and singer. When Donald Trump was about to be impeached the first time, Lizzo went viral with her impeachment tweet, where she wrote IM, then the peach emoji, then MENT. This is an instance of what linguists call the Rebus principle, which was used in the early development of the world's first writing system. Basically, this is the idea that, to have concrete symbols to represent something abstract, you take the sound of something that is concrete ("peach") that resembles the abstract thing. Lizzo didn't know she was using something that's been around for five and a half thousand years, but it just shows how inventive we all are.

ON: In 2015, the Oxford English Dictionary chose the crying-laughing emoji as its word of the year. What are the implications of this?

VE: There was a huge outcry, with some writers saying that it's ridiculous for an emoji to be a word. I think a lot of people still assume that an emoji is the equivalent of an adolescent grunt, but that's absolutely not the case. Use of emoji makes people better communicators in the digital space. For example, according to surveys conducted by Match.com, people who frequently use emoji get more dates. They have more sex. They claim to have better quality sex. And it's not because if you use an emoji, you get more sex—if only it were. It's because using emoji makes us more effective communicators and, by using them, we build emotional resonance in an online space. When you use these kinds of tools, you're replicating the body language you would otherwise use in a real dating context.

29

WASH OUT
The stubborn unsexiness of laundry.

We are truly living in the wellness age. Everything from what we eat and how we sleep to the way we fold our clothes has been rebranded as an opportunity to practice self-care. The wellness industry, estimated to be worth $1.5 trillion, or the GDP of Brazil, will sell you everything you need to live well. Yet washing clothes—a task so central to domestic life—stubbornly remains a chore.

How has it resisted *wellnessification*? Perhaps it's just because it's so unpopular—doing the laundry consistently ranks in surveys as people's least favorite household task. Or else it's because the wellness hive mind has failed to market such decidedly unglamorous tasks as sorting lights from darks or hanging out damp washing as being a vital part of your personal care regime.

But there is something to be said for this simple task even if it doesn't fit into our relentless drive for self-improvement. Pairing socks or ironing shirts offers a moment in a hectic day when you can stop and let your mind wander. And as you listen to the washing machine chugging away, you can always reflect on how the laundry day, with its hours of sweating and scrubbing, once meant something a lot more literal than it does now.

WORDS
GEORGE UPTON
PHOTOS
JULES SLUTSKY
ROMAIN LAPRADE

There is a style of language that is increasingly common on social media. Most often it takes the form of an extended caption disclosing some personal experience or asking banal questions that invite others to respond: Who else hates Mondays? What are you grateful for today? What's on your obsession list at the moment? Because this style of caption invites likes and replies, it presumes an audience is present, but it's not always clear who the intended audience is—particularly when the poster isn't a blue-ticked public figure, but a friend or acquaintance.

This conversational style first emerged among influencers, whose very "influence" stems from the active community their profiles attract. Even while influencers may hawk housewares, bath products or baby clothes, they are more authentic and more believable (although not always more trustworthy) than actors in traditional advertising. In a 1972 essay on advertising, the critic John Berger described this paradox: The more convincingly that ads convey "the pleasure of bathing in a warm, distant sea," the more the viewer "will become aware that he is hundreds of miles away from that sea." Influencers compress this distance by inviting users to see a real person living a "real" life.

Over the past few years, the conventions of influencer speak have been adopted by people who have nothing to sell. A telltale sign of its migration is the elongated caption. One acquaintance I follow on Instagram has started posting pictures with captions written like profound revelations. A blurred mirror selfie in front of an unmade bed is accompanied by a caption that reads: "It's really common for us to frame creativity through the lens of productivity and push ourselves too hard." The post has 31 likes.

It's curious that people seem to have unconsciously adopted a linguistic style whose purpose was born from advertising products. Of course, nobody would speak like actors in a commercial, but influencer speak seems both less obvious and more authentic. Still, the unreality of this style is occasionally exposed. Just as Instagram isn't a place for photos of dirty bathrooms, captions that discuss personal subjects can also fall flat. When users caption a photo "It's OK to not feel OK," for example, they draw attention to the inauthenticity of the form—the reality that nobody would speak like this in real life.

WORDS
HETTIE O'BRIEN

Photograph: BOCCA® BAROCCA – Performance for Gufram on the 50th anniversary of the BOCCA® sofa, with Elena Rivoltini, directed by Fabio Cherstich.

CAPTION CONTEST
On influencer speak.

CREATIVE BLOCK
An NFT primer.

Why would anyone pay $600,000 for a cat meme, downloaded millions of times, and easily accessible to all on the internet? What does it say about our yearning to purchase and possess that one collector was willing to shell out thousands of dollars for a few-second clip of LeBron James slam-dunking?

NFTs (the abbreviation stands for "non-fungible token") are unique digital assets bought with cryptocurrency (Bitcoin, Ethereum or Dogecoin, for example). In some cases, such as memes, the images are widely accessible, and the purchase doesn't halt their circulation and use. Twitter founder Jack Dorsey's first-ever tweet from 2006—"just setting up my twttr"—is now valued at $2.5 million (1630.6 Ethereum). In creating a tokenized version of the tweet, he gave the buyer digital rights of ownership.

So what's the draw? Until recently, NFTs existed within their own ecosystem. There were "NFT superstars," such as the Cryptopunks project—a 2017 work consisting of 10,000 AI-generated pixel-art portraits. But over the past 12 months, they have invaded the art world, mainstream media and dinner table discussions. Christie's, the global auction house, has come in for a slice of the pie; in March, they sold their first purely digital artwork—Beeple's jpeg file "Everydays: The First 5000 Days"—for $69 million, the highest price paid for an NFT at the time. It lit the wick for the future potential of this new art world.

For artists, NFTs are understandably exciting: Contemporary artists rarely get the chance to express themselves with an entirely new market, medium and consumer base. But what does their popularity say about the consumers at the other end of the transaction?[1] Is our desire to possess that which is readily accessible and available a metaphor for our obsession with ownership?

Why buy *things* when we can own the intangible? The internet is a home of sorts, so it is entirely fathomable that people want to own some of its assets. Whether or not we can compare NFTs to high art is, perhaps, not relevant: Their fast uptake and boom is a strong reminder of how, ultimately, the market dominates the art world.

(1) The irrationality of financial bubbles has a long history: In 1637, a speculative frenzy for rare tulip bulbs in the Netherlands sent prices soaring—and collapsing dramatically—within just a few short months.

WORDS
AINDREA EMELIFE
PHOTO
SÉBASTIEN BAERT

NIKOLAJ HANSSON

WORDS
JAMES CLASPER
PHOTO
CECILIE JEGSEN

An introduction to courtside cool.

"Tennis is a stop-and-start sport," says Nikolaj Hansson, who founded the Copenhagen-based Palmes earlier this year. A menswear brand with roots in tennis culture, Palmes was born of Hansson's interest in the sport's versatile wardrobe. "What I like about tennis clothing is that the polo shirt that you wear on court can also be worn to work," he says.

JAMES CLASPER: Have you always been into tennis?

NIKOLAJ HANSSON: Not at all. Growing up, I played tennis once or twice when I was on holiday. I never felt it was for me. I had this preconceived notion—one that's still relevant—that you need to come from the upper echelons of society to play tennis. When you say tennis, people think Wimbledon. They think white clothes, they think elite. That was somewhat ingrained in my mind, too.

JC: How did Palmes come about?

NH: I started playing tennis again a year ago and realized there wasn't anything in the world of tennis that I recognized or that reflected who I was and what I was into. In tennis, you have these performance-based brands, which are all about being the best, or you have legacy brands, which are very nostalgic, very upper-class and more about the heritage of tennis. There was nothing that had a more contemporary touch. I felt I could make something for people who were into the same things as me, who were interested in architecture, design, fashion and art.

JC: What do you like about tennis?

NH: Tennis is solely about what you do on court. And it's such a mental game. If you're not present, it doesn't matter how much you've trained; you're going to lose. I've also realized how amazing the culture is. Compared to a number of other sports, there are so many layers to tennis, culturally and historically. With Palmes, it's about passing on the feeling I have about tennis to more people and about using the brand to drive awareness of the sport. It's very much about showing that tennis can be for everyone. If I can just get one person to fall in love with it as much as I have, that'd be great.

JC: Is there a particular item that reflects that ethos?

NH: Many people find sports coats to be quite serious, somewhat stiff even, so our woolen sports coat has a slightly boxier fit, allowing you to wear a hooded sweatshirt underneath it on your way to the court. And the label on the inside has an illustration by a good friend of mine, which gives it a more contemporary feel.

JC: What was your design approach?

NH: I wanted to do something that wasn't exactly timeless—because timeless can be boring—but that had longevity and quality. All of the garments have been designed for at least four to six seasons, with subtle, understated details that make them relevant every single day—but not so much that they become irrelevant after six months.

JC: Finally, what's in the name?

NH: It comes from *jeu de paume*—a ball game that people in France used to play with the palm of their hands. I didn't want people to be able to tell where the brand is from. You can easily get put in a box—"Oh, this is a Scandinavian brand"—and Palmes is not about where it's from, it's about the feeling of the tennis.

ZONING PLAN
A route out of post-pandemic languishing.

Back in April 2021, psychologist Adam Grant put his finger on an enigma of the coronavirus pandemic. The health crisis had been dragging on for more than a year but there was light at the end of the tunnel—the terrible winter peak had passed, vaccines were being rolled out quickly, and the prospect of seeing family, hugging loved ones, and going on vacation was on the horizon. So why, Grant found himself asking, did we all feel so *blah*?

In an article for *The New York Times* that quickly went viral, Grant explains that this sense of stagnation and emptiness he felt is called languishing. He describes it as "the neglected middle child of mental health": we're not depressed—we can still get out of bed in the morning, keep up with our responsibilities around the house, go to work—but neither are we flourishing, as psychologists term mental and physical well-being. For most people, languishing will just mean an absence of enthusiasm or a drop in productivity, though it is also thought to be a risk factor in developing serious mental illness.

If you do find yourself struggling to get out of bed in the morning or lacking a sense of purpose, Grant suggests the answer could be found in something called *flow*.

Flow is the state of being completely engrossed in a task to the point that you don't notice time passing. Coined by Mihaly Csikszentmihalyi in 1975, it has long been understood as a way of finding enjoyment and fulfillment in life. You may have already found flow without realizing it—Kate Sweeny, a professor of psychology at the University of California, Riverside, suggests that the boom in baking and gardening during lockdown was the result of an instinctive drive to seek out flow.

You could find flow playing video games or doing the dishes, reading, or finally defuzzing your sweaters—it's not important whether it's ultimately productive or useful; just as long as you are *in the zone*, each action or idea flowing seamlessly and almost without conscious thought. It's a process Csikszentmihalyi likens to playing jazz.

This emphasis on the process rather than the end result has implications for how we work as well. Studies consistently find that we work better—and gain a greater sense of satisfaction—when we focus on one task rather than switching quickly between several different ones. And instead of evaluating our careers by whether we are achieving our grand ambitions, an emphasis on more day-to-day achievements, on finding flow as we work, is much more likely to help us grow in confidence and stay motivated.

Reaching a flow state won't necessarily mean you suddenly find yourself flourishing. But whether you are languishing or not, as well as offering a route out of a post-pandemic malaise, finding flow could be the key to a more creative, productive, and meaningful life.

Speedmaster Moonwatch by OMEGA

WORDS
GEORGE UPTON
PHOTO
CHRISTIAN MØLLER ANDERSEN

HOLY MACARONI
The architects searching for perfect pasta.

WORDS
ALEX ANDERSON
PHOTO
ROMAIN LAPRADE

STARTERS

During the early 20th century, a group of Italian Futurist artists and architects decreed there was to be "no more spaghetti for Italians." Because pasta making called for speed and scientific precision, Futurist cuisine could not tolerate the slow, assured process of kneading dough and forming it into ancestral shapes perfectly attuned to regional sauces. Nor could it countenance the quaintly colloquial names carried by each pasta shape—"little tongues" (linguini), "knuckles" (gnocchi), "little ears" (orecchiette). *The Futurist Cookbook*, published in 1932, contained a recipe for ice cream on the moon—but no noodles.

Any loyal Futurist would be dismayed by more recent events. In the later 20th century, artists, designers and architects came to view pasta as a fascinating design *objet*. In 1983, Barilla, the world's largest pasta producer, hired industrial designer Giorgetto Giugiaro to devise a new noodle shape. He presented the world with "marille," an elaborately curved and scalloped extrusion meant to evoke the sea. It was, by all accounts, "a total failure"—gastronomically and commercially. The next year, rival pasta brand Panzani asked designer Philippe Starck to try his hand at the same task. He produced an elaborate penne noodle with wings. "Because American and French people always overcook pasta," he explained, "I made two wings that have a double thickness, so when you overcook it, eighty percent of the pasta is still al dente." Starck's pasta failed too.

It is, understandably, hard for designers to resist the allure of a food that so beautifully embodies the concept of form. Architect George Legendre's mathematical explorations of traditional pasta shapes in *Pasta by Design* offer proof of the vast and subtle possibility of noodles. Its catalog of more than 300 traditional pastas, arranged in families, reveals the elegant architectural lines, spirals and helixes of capellini, colonne Pompeii and gigli.

For designers, this variability is a call to invent. So, not long ago, designer Kenya Hara assembled an astounding exhibition of new pasta shapes devised by eight different Japanese architectural firms. Displayed at 20 times actual size, each shape sought to transcend the simplicity of semolina, egg yolk, oil and salt. "Wave-Ripple-Loop-Surf" by Tadasu Ohe presented undulating disks of pasta to accompany salmon, mussels and scallops swimming in butter. To form "Maccheroni" by Atelier Zo, pinch a small cylinder of dough with both thumbs and forefingers, then twist. Cook and sauce with a simple marinara.

Despite designers' whimsical efforts to come up with new pasta shapes, it seems unlikely that they will improve on linguini, farfalle or gnocchi. But why stop trying?[1] The Futurists' absurd prohibition of pasta must hold no sway over the possibility that some designer just might fashion a new noodle that everyone wants to eat.

---

(1) In April 2021, Dan Pashman, host of the podcast *The Sporkful*, launched a new pasta shape called cascatelli (Italian for "waterfalls"), with Sfoglini. He spent three years designing a shape that would maximize "sauceability, forkability and toothsinkability."

There's something thrilling and transgressive about looking through the window of a stranger's house: It's a rare insight into how other people really live their lives when they think no one is watching. Voyeuristic as it may seem, there's something to be gained from seeing and being seen in our private spaces—a sense of communion with strangers, that feels particularly necessary in big cities.

In Alfred Hitchcock's 1954 thriller *Rear Window*, this enforced closeness becomes a metaphor for the voyeurism of urban confinement, and the moral responsibility—or lack thereof—between neighbors. Jeff, a wounded documentary photographer, takes to looking out of his Manhattan apartment window and studying his neighbors to pass the time until he can work again. He observes a composer obsessively playing the same song over and over, a ballet dancer who dances rather than walks around her apartment and a lonely woman who holds dinner parties with imaginary guests. He eventually becomes suspicious that one neighbor has murdered his wife, and the unwritten rule of nonintervention reaches its breaking point: "I've seen it through that window," he says, trying to convince some visitors of his theory. He pieces together the evidence needed for a search warrant, the piece of paper that allows the otherwise unpardonable act of entering another's home.

The cultural trope of looking through a window trades on the idea that it's a morally questionable act. But what happens when the secretive element is removed? In the Netherlands, looking into people's windows is embedded in the culture. The Calvinist religious society, which began in the 16th century with Protestant reformer John Calvin, expounded the idea that citizens should not have anything to hide from God and therefore from their neighbors, and curtains became associated with an anti-religious spirit. To this day, you can wander the rows of canal houses in Amsterdam and see hardly a single curtain. Looking in through windows has become something of a pastime for those strolling along the canals at night.

With countless new ways to "spy" on one another in contemporary society, the window is a less vital channel into the lives of others. But few things carry the subversive thrill of peeking into an unknown kitchen or living room, even if you're more likely to pick up interior design tips than the key to solving a murder.

INSIDE OUT
The opaque allure of window watching.

WORDS
BAYA SIMONS
PHOTO
SALVA LÓPEZ

Book endorsements are the fuel that keeps the publishing industry's hype machine in motion. This perhaps explains why some better-known authors allegedly knock them out without even reading the novel they're praising. Writing in *The Guardian* a few years ago, the novelist Nathan Filer revealed that he had received 42 unsolicited proofs in the six months after winning the Costa Book of the Year prize—each accompanied by hyperbolic prose from the publishers, who clearly hoped that some authors would repeat their praise verbatim in quotes for the cover.

Whether the words originate from marketing teams or time-strapped authors, the effusive and occasionally unintelligible language of book blurbs is prolific. Frank McCourt, the author of *Angela's Ashes*, seems to believe that three separate books will make you want to "claw yourself with pleasure." Nicole Krauss, author of four novels, wrote that reading David Grossman's *To the End of the Land* was to be "taken apart, undone, touched at the place of your own essence." Unencumbered by their editors, writers seem to be competing to find new, increasingly outlandish ways of describing each other's work.

Writing presciently about the practice of advanced book blurbing in 1991, the controversial American academic Camille Paglia said it was "absolutely appalling, because it means that they send your book around to your friends, they scratch your back, and you scratch theirs. This is part of the coziness of the profession that I think has just been pernicious."

Of course, it's not just writers who are in the habit of generating a secret, nonsensical lexicon. Such linguistic codes—where words means very little except to those in the know—span all sectors. They pop up in the language of HR ("self-starter," "agent for change") and tech ("ecosystem," "ideation"). After all, codes are simply a way of gatekeeping—of creating a tribe and recognizing those who do and don't belong. Collegial solidarity is well and good, but not if it comes at the expense of useful communication. It seems odd that publishing is so insistent on this particular form of industry jargon, because book blurbs are ultimately outward facing, designed to communicate to a general audience rather than to an in-crowd. As far back as 1936, George Orwell warned that readers could in fact be put off by the fear that they may not "shriek with delight" when encountering a novel.

WORDS
DEBIKA RAY
PHOTO
NOÉ SENDAS

Artwork: *Charlotte Suite (I)*, 2015

COVER STORY
Inside the book blurb racket.

THE GENE GENIE

WORDS
BELLA GLADMAN
COLLAGE
NICOLA KLOOSTERMAN

In conversation with a de-extinction biologist.

Many kids will go through a dinosaur-obsessed phase in their childhood, but few follow scientist Ben Novak's path. Novak, who once won a youth science fair with a project about bringing the dodo back, now leads the development of scientific programs at Revive & Restore, a nonprofit whose mission is the genetic rescue of endangered and extinct species. Having grown up in western North Dakota, where he witnessed the bison, bighorn sheep and elks that had been reintroduced to Theodore Roosevelt National Park, Novak is currently working on a project to use genetic engineering to resurrect the passenger pigeon, which was native to North America and overhunted, leading to extinction in 1914.

BELLA GLADMAN: What can you tell me about de-extinction?

BEN NOVAK: De-extinction has been going on for centuries. In different areas, humans already work to reintroduce lost species—such as beavers to the UK, and European bison to Spain. Regarding the passenger pigeon project, you can't clone birds in the same way as mammals, so we'd need to find out how to do that first. Even if we aren't able to revive the passenger pigeon, the research we would gain along the way would be invaluable to so many other disciplines.

BG: What do you do at Revive & Restore?

BN: We foster the innovation and adoption of genomic biotechnologies for wildlife conservation. One part is sequencing genomes to find out more about existing and endangered species. For example, horseshoe crab blood is used for vaccine testing—if you've ever had a vaccine, you owe your life to a horseshoe crab. Genome sequencing has allowed us to recreate their blood's useful properties, so they no longer have to be harvested and exploited. We also work with advanced reproductive technologies, like artificial insemination, reintroducing genetic diversity into dwindling populations like the black-footed ferret, to make them more resistant to disease and inbreeding.

BG: Gene editing has a mixed reputation.

BN: It's been used already in American chestnut trees. Formerly abundant, they nearly died out from a fungal disease carried by the Asian horse chestnut when it was imported in the late 1800s. William Powell and his team at SUNY College of Environmental Science and Forestry found an immunity gene in other trees, and inserted it into American chestnuts to make them disease-resistant. Local communities have embraced this: One of the Indigenous tribes, the Eastern Band of Cherokee Indians in North Carolina, signed an agreement in 2021 that they will plant these engineered trees on their land. They're getting back a piece of their culture that's been gone for a hundred years. It's never too late to save a species.

BG: How fair is the comparison to *Jurassic Park*?

BN: It's an entertaining tale but very different from what we're trying to do. First, dinosaurs no longer have a place in this world. Instead, we're trying to revive the creatures that were killed by human greed, like passenger pigeons. Second, we would have no intention of putting them in a park as an amusement—our ultimate goal is to let these animals live, and leave them alone entirely.

IT'S KNOT YOU
The curious history of the sweater curse.

There are many activities people are superstitious about: breaking mirrors, spilling salt and walking under ladders, to name a few. In the world of knitting, it is the "sweater curse" that strikes fear. Also known as "the curse of the love sweater" or "the curse of the boyfriend sweater," it works like this: A person knits a sweater for their partner and it leads to the unraveling of their relationship. For many ardent knitters, this isn't just superstition, but a phenomenon confirmed in the anecdotes of friends and online forums.[1]

Knitting your partner a sweater as an act of devotion has a time-honored lineage. In her 2007 book *Son of Stitch 'n Bitch*, Debbie Stoller writes that "in [19th-cenutry] Holland it was traditional for a bride to begin knitting [the] sweater for her betrothed on the day the wedding date was set." The book also mentions similar customs in Britain at the time. "The future bride of a fisherman began knitting this special sweater as soon as she was engaged—and not a moment before," Stoller writes. The belief that knitting your partner a sweater before marriage can lead to the relationship's ultimate demise is more recent, however: It has grown in popularity over the last decade to the extent that internet forums are awash with messages by heartbroken knitters. "So I'm halfway through making his, and he broke up with me. Now I'm left with half a sweater and I can confirm that it's a curse," writes one devastated Reddit user on making a Harry Potter–themed Christmas pullover for her partner.

This sort of bad luck isn't unique to knitting. According to Stephen Crabbe, senior lecturer in Applied Linguistics and Translation at the University of Portsmouth, getting a tattoo of your lover's name is believed by many in the industry to doom the relationship. "According to Premier Laser Clinic after a five-year study, the most regretted tattoo (and the one most frequently removed) by customers at their clinics was an ex's name," he writes in *The Conversation*.

One obvious reason why these acts of devotion may spell disaster is that too grand a gesture too soon can force couples to rethink their relationship. As the Pulitzer Prize–winning author Alison Lurie once wrote in *The New Yorker*: "A handmade sweater is typically thick, elastic, and clingy: it suggests that the woman who is making it wants to surround its recipient and enclose him. To be presented with such a garment is a signal to a man that its maker has serious plans for him. If he is not ready for this, the gift will embarrass him and may frighten him away."

Ultimately, time is not on the knitter's side: A sweater can take several months to complete, a tattoo lasts forever. No wonder a significant proportion of relationships end up souring in the meantime. To hedge your bets, start with a scarf and work up from there.

WORDS
PRECIOUS ADESINA
PHOTO
CHRISTIAN HEIKOOP

(1) In a 2005 poll by one such forum, the website *Knitters Review*, 15% of active knitters responded that they had experienced the sweater curse firsthand, and 41% considered it a possibility that should be taken seriously.

45

STARTERS

JON BATISTE

WORDS
CHARLES SHAFAIEH
PHOTOS
JUSTIN FRENCH

The band leader on his genre-busting year.

Jon Batiste's fifth studio album, *We Are*, is by turns jubilant and tender. The same description applies to the musician himself, who speaks with strangers as if they were longtime friends and often breaks into song without prompting. The 34-year-old son of a storied New Orleans music family has many reasons for joy of late.[1] Best known as the band leader for *The Late Show with Stephen Colbert*, he recently attracted a younger audience with Pixar's animated hit *Soul*, whose jazz pianist protagonist's fingers are modeled on his own. Just days before our interview, he, along with co-composers Trent Reznor and Atticus Ross, won an Academy Award for their score for the film. Batiste doesn't restrict his talents to the screen, the studio or the concert hall however. Music, he believes, belongs in the street, which he demonstrates in "love riots"—at once public parades and spontaneous social interventions that occur as finales to his performances or whenever he and his friends feel compelled to meet and play. In June 2020, thousands followed him across New York City in marches supporting Black Lives Matter, as those with instruments created an ecstatic soundscape of spiritual and emancipatory anthems.

CHARLES SHAFAIEH: *We Are* continues your established practice of breaking apart genres. Why is eliminating these market-imposed categories vital to you?

JON BATISTE: There are no different forms of music. There's only music. For this album, the first thing we did in the studio with the band was record the Justin Bieber song "Let Me Love You." I like the song, but it was also to get us outside the box of thinking about making music together, the way we're used to and the way that people expect. As an artist, you always want to push yourself to find new territories. That's why I'm against

genres. They limit artistic expression, thus they limit human expression. And if you limit the expression of the artist, then it no longer becomes art. It becomes a form of virtue signaling for a lifestyle or a brand—something that eats itself.

CS: Does taking music out into the streets also redefine the concert experience?

JB: The rawest form of music was on display for centuries before it was a commodity. We need to get back to that because there's a lot of wisdom, joy and truth in music exchange and in using music as something that connects people to the past as well as preserves history for the future. Playing in the street is one way to open people up to music in its rawest form and see it in action. I call that social music. New Orleans is one of the few places in the world where there is still social music. There's music for when someone passes away, for almost every different occasion within a community. It's not a thing that most people consider a normal part of life beyond entertainment value. It's few and far between—in Cuba, Brazil and different parts of the [American] South.

CS: You've brought social music to New York City, beginning when, at Juilliard, you performed in the subway with your band, Stay Human. Are subway crowds a distinctive audience?

JB: At college, I've had really varied performance experiences: playing with jazz greats Roy Hargrove, Abbey Lincoln and Wynton Marsalis, and with Lenny Kravitz and Prince; recording an album with Chad Smith and Bill Laswell; and these subway hits. Everything fed into everything else, and I noticed more what connects every aspect of performance, not the differences. At every performance, people at a certain point collectively decide whether to be open or closed to an experience. In the subway, they're not expecting the experience. At an arena, there's great anticipation. At a jazz venue, there's a certain type of listening. The connectivity of all these things is that everybody gets on a wavelength—or they don't. In the subway, what's special is that you get people who are not expecting to be on the same wavelength to resonate on the same frequency. It feels like you've transmuted the energy in a space. A lot of the time New Yorkers dread being there, and then, all of a sudden, it's a party, a jovial atmosphere, a space where there's community and social engagement.

CS: Your work also collapses time and space. It's a processional of sorts, in which you evoke composers and artists who have left us and call into the future to those not yet born.

JB: The greatest power of music is time travel. There's not a way of doing that in many other art forms as immediately as in music. Imagine if you take Bach's influence and bind it with someone who wasn't around in his time, like Kendrick Lamar or Ali Farka Touré. What other art form can do that with such immediacy and impact? That's what the greatest artists have done—channel people who came before them while doing something new in the present which will then inspire generations to come. That's the definition of a musical icon. Music as an art form is endless and an opportunity to mine the collective human consciousness without losing your own unique perspective on it.

CS: That interplay between the group and the individual seems like a jazz sensibility—respecting the group but celebrating the independent voice.

JB: Jazz is an example of how the individual voice can be just as important as the democratic group function, how co-creation can be just as important as individuality. Like what we struggle with in democracy, it's about individual freedoms, freedom of speech, but also constant compromise and collective bargaining to coexist peacefully. It's a paradox of objectives. Jazz is not really a form of music. It's a philosophy tied to a sociocultural phenomenon. Jazz hands, finger snaps, cool clubs—that's poor marketing of what jazz is. It has such deep roots in the Black experience and in slavery, the original sin of America. It takes different forms of culture from around the globe and incorporates them into the experience, which is the most quintessentially American anything can be. It's an art form that, for the first time in history, is based in the past and the present, and it's the most modern form of creating the future because it's happening every second as you watch and listen to it, right in front of you.

Listen to Duke Ellington's "Diminuendo and Crescendo in Blue" and Paul Gonsalves on tenor saxophone playing a 27-chorus solo. You can hear in the recording that wasn't set up to be 27 choruses long. It's just that the audience kept shouting, and he kept going higher and higher. It became this feedback loop of energy. This is a piece that is very through-composed, but there's this section that allows for this engagement with the audience. That's one of the great innovations of jazz. You allow for the audience to be a part of the experience.[2]

CS: The audience can propel you to unexpected places of discovery. What do you feel is pushing into your consciousness right now, about which you're hungry to know more?

JB: I find it's most illuminating to determine your course of study based on extremes. That will help you make connections to disparate things, which are, to me, the lifeblood of the artist. If you can find a way to connect being an auto mechanic with writing a song, or the hierarchy of the military to watercolors, that's exciting. It opens up new ways of thinking about what it is that you do. I'm always inspired at the end of that process.

(1)   Batiste comes from a New Orleans musical dynasty. His father, Michael, was a bassist who performed with Jackie Wilson and Isaac Hayes.
(2)   According to Pete Docter, who co-directed *Soul*, Batiste created his jazz compositions for the movie to be "user-friendly," so that "people who aren't jazz fans will still appreciate and be moved by the music."

Alongside his many other pursuits, Batiste is co-artistic director of the National Jazz Museum in Harlem and has been actively involved in the museum's programming since 2009.

Michèle LAMY:

Words
ROBERT ITO

TE HIGH PRIESTESS OF PARIS.

Photography
LUC BRAQUET

Styling: Gill Linton. Set Design: Déborah Sadoun. Hair & Makeup: Jean-Charles Perrier

Michèle Lamy is in a hotel room in Venice along the Grand Canal, sunlight streaming in through sheer curtained windows, the calls of seabirds in the air. In addition to being one of the world's most genre-confounding creatives, Lamy is also one of its most idiosyncratic dressers. On various occasions, she has worn sphinxlike headdresses and suction cups on her forehead; enormous, sculptural jackets paired with short shorts and foot-tall platform boots (for British *Vogue*'s "Inside the Wardrobe" series); and a purse fashioned out of an eerily lifelike replica of her husband's head.[1]

So I ask what she's wearing today. "I'm wearing a cashmere sweater," she tells me, "but upside down." Her arms are through the sleeves, but the neck hole is dangling down by her waist. "I'm wearing a bodysuit on one side," she continues, "and a shirt on the other." Since we're on Zoom, she stands up so that I can see how the fabrics and pieces are arrayed. Atop her head is what looks like an elfin skullcap, but it's actually a face mask created by the fashion designer Rick Owens, Lamy's husband and business partner, who is behind her in the hotel room, working at a small wooden desk. On every finger are rings atop rings. "I'm always wearing the rings," she says. Stacks of bracelets click click click every time she moves her arms.

Lamy is in town for the opening of the Architecture Biennale. When she was here in 2015, she commandeered a barge once used to haul trucks to create Bargenale, a floating house party/art project/communal dining hall that included a recording studio and onboard restaurant, and attracted guests like the American rapper A$AP Rocky and the English musician James Lavelle.[2] In 2019, she returned with *LAMYLAND: What Are We Fighting For?*, a boxing installation that featured nine punching bags designed for the show by a host of international artists.

The theme of this year's Venice Biennale is "How Will We Live Together?" which seems like an appropriate topic after the year we've all muddled through. "It's a question I've personally been asking," Lamy says. "How do we live together? It's very complicated, when it should not be."

This year, Lamy is at the Biennale as a spectator, but she hopes to return to the city at the end of August to participate in a "floating cinema" planned by the curator Paolo Rosso. There will be a big screen floating in the middle of the Venetian Lagoon, she tells me, accessible only by small fishing boats, and there will likely be great parties along the docks. Lamy has been asked to curate her own 90-minute program for the aquatic film festival.

I am speaking to Lamy from Los Angeles. She tells me she'll be visiting in July to shoot some things for the Lagoon project, although what exactly—maybe a movie, maybe some videos—she's still not sure. "You know that I lived for 30 years in LA?" she asks

(1)   Lamy carried the prosthetic head to attend the Rick Owens Fall Winter 2020 show at the Palais de Tokyo in Paris. "It has everything I need: my phone, money and cigarettes," she told *Vogue* at the time.

(2)   A$AP Rocky has been a friend and collaborator of Lamy's since 2008. She shot his *At. Long. Last. ASAP* album cover, on which he wears a ring gifted by Lamy.

me. During her tenure, Lamy was a near-mythic figure in the city, heralded for her sense of style, her parties, her ability to move between subcultures and peoples. At 77, she is still a presence here, collaborating with and encouraging the town's rising artists, designers and creatives.

Lamy was born in Jura, France, in 1944. After boarding school, where she boned up on her English by reading the works of Henry Miller ("the books are very sexy"), she worked as a cabaret dancer and took part in the May 1968 protests in Paris.[3] In the late 1970s, she moved to New York, hanging out at places like Studio 54. Her brother told her that she didn't have enough money "to be cool in New York," but that Los Angeles was a different story. "He said it was like New York on the Riviera." Lamy was drawn to Los Angeles by writers like Susan Sontag and Joan Didion, who immortalized and pilloried the city in many of her best-known works. "The music, the literature, everything was attracting me there," she says. She moved to the city in 1979.

> " I've always tried to put myself in situations of being with people you think you belong with, or that you want to belong with, or that surprise you."

At various times, Lamy headed up her own eponymous clothing company, and ran a retail store on Santa Monica Blvd called Too Soon To Know. Around 1991, she opened Les Deux Café, a legendary meeting place for the city's A-list actors, musicians and artists—everyone from Al Pacino and David Lynch to Lenny Kravitz and Madonna. Everything about the place was ostentatiously secretive, from its nondescript parking lot to its unmarked steel door. "When I built Les Deux Café, it was a parking lot," Lamy says. "And I said, 'I'm going to transform it into a garden.'" From there, the story morphs into something so magical and fortuitous—an empty lot metamorphosed into one of the city's most mythical hotspots—that it sounds like it all came about by happy chance. Of course, there was more to it than that. "I've been a hard worker, feeling the pain, so now, what you call chance, you make your own chance," she says. (Lamy's English often has a charming habit of going its own way.) She's also intensely curious, she says, with a "nomadic spirit" and so many places she'd still like to go. "Can you believe I did not go to Japan yet?" she asks. She hopes to go there soon. "I've always tried to put myself in situations of being with people you think you belong with, or that you want to belong with, or that surprise you."

(3) During Paris Fashion Week in 2019, Lamy returned to cabaret at Manko Paris. She performed twice, dressed entirely in boxing hand wraps, dancing with the artist Jean-Biche.

Lamy left Los Angeles in 2003. "We moved to Paris because Rick Owens had to move there," she says, using his entire name as if I might not know who he is, or that he's right behind her in the room, within earshot. (Owens came to Paris to serve as artistic director of the venerable French fur company Revillon.) But Lamy still loves Los Angeles, and quickly rattles off several spots she would take a first-time visitor to the area: the arts district downtown; the skatepark and boardwalk in Venice Beach; Palm Springs, where she once got her fingers tattooed; the fabled Chateau Marmont. "I would even take them to the Valley!" she says. When she talks to me about LA she adds, pointedly, "*where you are!*" I'm going back to LA, *where you are!* I was coming back from LA, *where you are.* It is an endearing point of connection from a woman who clearly misses the place.

Lamy's assistant, Janet Fischgrund, has arranged to have a copy of *Rick Owens Furniture*, a lovely coffee-table book from Rizzoli, messengered over to me from the Rick Owens clothing store in West Hollywood. For years, Lamy has collaborated with her husband on a furniture line, which tends more toward the artistic and the minimalist (a recent show at LA's Museum of Contemporary Art featured pieces constructed from marble, concrete and ox bone) than to the practical or cozy. The book is unlike nearly any other furniture book you might happen upon: part travelogue, with stops in Tuscany, Dubai, Montreal and the Dead Sea; part family photo album, with portraits of the couple by Danielle Levitt and Jean-Baptiste Mondino; part art book. A photo of an "antler stool" crafted from poured aluminum, with two horns where your buttocks would go, is next to a close-up of Lamy's front teeth, which feature several small diamonds embedded in the gold fillings.[4] There are pictures of toilets made of rock crystal, shots of cigarette butts and TV remotes in the couple's home, which is part of the five-storey building at the Place du Palais Bourbon (site of the French National Assembly building) where Owenscorp is headquartered, and candids of Lamy driving a forklift in one of their factories and walking in the snow of St. Moritz.

The captions in the books are one or two words long, so I ask Lamy to explain what's happening in a few of the photos. In one, labeled "Hollywood, December 1995," Lamy is standing in front of two enormous photographs that look like 1950s mug shots. Her left arm, adorned with a stack of bracelets, is on her hip; in her right hand is a cigarette, held aloft as if she were a glamorous figure advertising it. She looks like a model. "This picture was taken when I was building the Les Deux Café, and Rick had his studio across the street," she says. "That was his first [fashion line], it was not even a collection, then," she says. They both lived and worked at the studio. It was a time of intense creation for Owens and Lamy, she says, a "carnival time." "This is one of the more joyous pictures," she says. "And I think I look good in it."

> " I like to perform, the more people the better. If it's a bigger venue and a lot of people, I'm floating in the air!"

In another sequence of photos, labeled "Mons, Belgium, 2013," Lamy is looking intently at enormous slabs of marble. "This is in a quarry of black marble, the only one left between Belgium and France," she says. "You have to go 60 meters underground to see it. They take the marble with dynamite." She was there to find large, blemish-free slabs of marble for the Rick Owens furniture line, to be later fashioned into beds and chairs and tables, some weighing in the tons. Lamy learned quickly what to look for and how to find the most beautiful specimens ("no veins"), she says. Then she spins off into a series of stories about an enormous mosque in Abu Dhabi crafted out of white Sivec marble, and how black marble came to be black (something to do with coal), and how, now, "because we have to save the world," they and others are looking at "liquid stone," which, in the end, just sounds like concrete. "So that's another interesting story," she says. It is, in fact, several interesting stories, emerging one from the other and sometimes wrapping back into the original story, sometimes not, which is a pretty decent way of describing what it's like to talk to Lamy.

In another photo, captioned "Ebenisterie Dagorn, Saint-Fargeau-Ponthierry, April 2016," Lamy is pushing a broom across a factory floor. Surely there are others who could sweep up? "Perhaps everyone was on a truck going somewhere," she says. "But somebody has to do it." She considers. "Or perhaps I did it as a joke?"

(4) It was a shaman dentist in LA who first recommended that Lamy replace her mercury fillings with gold. "I want another one and then I want another one. You know how it is," she told *The Cut* in 2015.

Like all of us, Lamy's life and schedule has been upended by the pandemic. Even so, over the past year, she has made a short film with Kim Kardashian inspired by the tea party in Lewis Carroll's *Alice's Adventures in Wonderland*, cooked up honey and mustard chicken (using honey from her own bees) with the Bronx-based culinary collective Ghetto Gastro, and traveled to Milan with Owens, via a custom-designed tour bus, to help launch the Moncler + Rick Owens collection.[5] In other words, Lamy's not easing up a bit. Unlike artists who create a particular voice or style then find themselves stuck within it, Lamy continues to push boundaries and herself.

In the coming year or so, she hopes to go on tour again with LAVASCAR, a musical group she formed with her daughter, Scarlett Rouge, and Nico Vascellari, a Venice-based visual artist. The music is hard to describe, a mix of spoken word (Lamy performing the poems of Langston Hughes, Etel Adnan and others), and animal sounds (by Rouge). "It's a noise band," she explains. Planned gigs in Latvia and Georgia were scuttled last year because of the pandemic, but Lamy would like to begin performing again soon. "I like to perform, the more people the better," she says. In smaller places, "I could be a little self-conscious. But if it's a bigger venue and a lot of people, I'm floating in the air! I read my stories, and it's like I'm in the stories, one after the other that go somewhere. And Nico has a way with sort of primitive time, the drums, that I love, and then I can laugh as much as I can."

"With the laugh, you can express something without words."

The laugh is actually part of her performances, so much so that a curator, intrigued by her laugh, among other things, invited Lamy to come to Abu Dhabi and laugh there. She told her about a tradition among Bedouin tribesmen, where, during times of crisis, a person wise in such matters would read the laughter of someone in the hopes of gaining insights into the future. Lamy will do more than laugh there, of course, but just what and when is still up in the air. "When there was hard times, war, or disease, they would read the laugh, and they could tell from the laugh if things were going to turn the right way, or if you were going to be in pain some more time," she says. Lamy is unsure if someone will be there to read her laugh and, based on those sounds, foretell what is to come, but she's not closed to the idea. "We certainly remind people that, with the laugh, you can express something without words. And then perhaps somebody will also be able to figure out what's going to happen? And me, too."

(5)   Lamy and Kim Kardashian have collaborated on other occasions. During the pandemic, the two appeared on the cover of *AnOther* magazine alongside text messages they had exchanged during lockdown. "À demain, twin monkey," is how Lamy signs off the conversation.

Sunrise to sunset on the Catalonian coastline.

Photography
SALVA LÓPEZ
Styling
JUAN CAMILO
RODRÍGUEZ

(previous)   Matteo wears a shirt by DRIES VAN NOTEN and shorts by IAGO OTERO.
(top right)   Matteo wears a shirt by BOTTEGA VENETA.
(below)   He wears a coat by EDWARD CUMING and trousers by ARDUSSE.
(bottom   He wears a sweater by ARDUSSE and trousers and shorts by EDWARD CUMING.
right)

(below)   Towel from BON VENT.

Hair & Makeup
ANASTASIIA BABII
Production
ANTON BRIANSÓ
& POL MASIP

(previous)   Shawna wears a shirt and shorts by IAGO OTERO. Matteo wears a shirt by DRIES VAN NOTEN and shorts by IAGO OTERO. Both wear shoes by HEREU.
(top left)   Shawna wears a dress by KENZO and shoes by VERSACE.
(bottom   She wears a shirt by APRÈS SKI, shorts by IAGO OTERO and shoes by HEREU.
right)

(left)   Matteo wears an undershirt by VERSACE and a shirt by ARDUSSE.
(overleaf)   Shawna wears a coat by EDWARD CUMING and Matteo wears a jacket by DRIES VAN NOTEN and a shirt by ARDUSSE.

Models
MATTEO CORTELLARO &
SHAWNA BLACKBURN
at UNO Models
Locations
CAN CARRERAS & EMPÚRIES

Can Instagram
slideshows save
the world?

ESSAY:
THE INFOGRAPHIC
INDUSTRIAL
COMPLEX

Words
SARAH MANAVIS

Do you know what's happening in the Middle East? Maybe you want to understand microaggressions, impostor syndrome or the foundations of feminism. The good news is you can now find everything you need to know while scrolling Instagram.

Few social media trends in the last decade have taken hold quite as quickly as the made-for-Instagram infographic. These slideshows, usually shared on the Stories function of Instagram, where images disappear after 24 hours, are now an unavoidable part of the social media user experience.[1] They have been heralded as a creative new form of activism, one that is inherently tied to Instagram's functionality and its prioritizing of eye-catching visuals.

In the last year, though, communicating on the most complex issues of world politics and

The emergence of the infographic at the end of the 18th century was "almost destined," says Dr. Murray Dick, author of *The Infographic: A History of Data Graphics in News and Communications.* During the late Enlightenment period, more and more people were collecting and generating original data to use in textbooks, reference works and other academic publications. When the need for a clear, effective way to convey their findings arose, researchers turned to the new data visualizations that had been dreamed up by Scottish engineer and economist William Playfair, such as bar charts, pie charts and line graphs.

Many of those consuming infographics at the time had academic backgrounds in cartography, meaning they could comprehend highly complex diagrams. "The origins of infographics are not as a simple, universal language that could

" The origins of infographics are not as a simple, universal language that could communicate to anyone."

social justice via a handful of pastel-hued slides has come to feel overly simplistic; failing to tackle complex issues with the nuance they require. While some can be useful and educational, these infographics have increasingly been accused of flattening discourse or being laced with obvious bias. For example, early on in the COVID pandemic, an authoritative "data pack" infographic emphasizing the mildness of most infections was shared by celebrities including Kendall Jenner, who has over 166 million Instagram followers. Scientists quickly pointed out the flaws in its presentation: It ignored the risk of hospitals being overwhelmed, long COVID and the possibility of younger people infecting the elderly, but that didn't stop it from doing the rounds online.

Though the surge of infographics on social media feels deeply modern, using them as a tool for argument is part of a centuries-old pattern.

communicate to anyone," Dick points out. "They were very much bound up in an elite discourse—elite people talking to other elite people about elite issues." There were some exceptions, however, such as the beautiful, intricate infographics made by W.E.B. Du Bois, which plotted how African Americans remained oppressed by institutional racism more than three decades after the end of slavery.

(1)   These slideshows have now become ripe for parody. In spring 2021, when the attempted formation of the European Super League was grabbing headlines, several meme accounts published faux-sincere infographics with headlines such as "What's happening in football and what you can do to help."

(2)   The term "woke washing" is used to describe how some corporations use infographics related to social justice. For example, a fast fashion brand posting resources on racial equity and feminism can obscure the fact that they are actively harming marginalized people through unfair labor practices.

The true explosion of infographics as a tool of mass communication began at the turn of the 20th century. Newspapers and magazines began publishing infographics regularly, realizing they could draw in more readers if they accompanied written articles with a compelling infographic. As more illustrators got involved, symbols and text were used to enliven dry data and to capture the attention of a broader audience—representing worker numbers with drawings of men, for example. This era also gave rise to infographics as tools for political persuasion: They were often used to show the reasoning behind one side of a debate, such as a chart explaining how tuberculosis could be contained by comparing the rates of infection under self-isolation against those without quarantine in place.

" Frankly, when you have lots of people just creating these things for the sake of it, it does create noise. And it does also end up creating misinformation."

Infographics, particularly those made by newspapers, had a reputation throughout the 20th century of being "often unabashedly propagandistic," Dick says. However, parts of the industry have been thoroughly professionalized over the decades since: Standardized data visualizations are now created by dedicated news outlets (think statistical analysis sites like *FiveThirtyEight* or the obsessive prediction maps we see during elections).[3]

But while the professionalization of infographics was occurring within traditional media, the aughts and early 2010s saw a new type of creator begin to emerge: the general public. "Each new wave [of creation] is always related to technologies that provide the means for people to create infographics," explains Sandra Rendgen, author of *History of Information Graphics*. "Around 2007, the internet was widely available—everyone had a personal computer. Therefore, everybody had the means of graphic production."[4]

(3)   There are, of course, many infographic creators who apply equally rigorous standards to the content they produce for social media. For example, the data journalist Mona Chalabi regularly publishes her sources and explains how she turns raw data into eye-catching illustration.

During this time, we saw the beginnings of what we now associate with modern Instagram infographics: homemade diagrams, usually arguing a political point of view, often without citation and often misleadingly reductive. Until just a few years ago, these infographics largely existed on small blogs, unlikely to be seen by more than a handful of people.

Then, Instagram tweaked its functionality in a way that would dramatically change the distribution of infographics by allowing posts—the photos or videos uploaded to a user's grid, often accompanied by an explanatory text caption—to be shared through Stories. This small, technical change motivated people to share information in a visual format and paved the way for the current infographics boom that arguably began in the summer of 2020, when there was a sharp rise in educational posts covering topics such as systematic racism, charting Black deaths in police custody and relaying statistics around arrests related to race.

But much like the traditional print media in the early 20th century, explains Juliette Cezzar, a professor of communication design at the New School's Parsons School of Design, influencers realized that they could use infographics to gain clout.

Without the understanding needed to represent statistical data accurately in graphic form, this incentive has sometimes led influencers to share reductive, hastily compiled or lopsided versions of the truth. For example, several infographics disseminated during the Black Lives Matter protests touted the same statistic: that more white Americans are killed each year by the police than Black Americans. However, these posts omitted the data per capita—which reveals that Black Americans are actually killed by police at twice the rate of white Americans. "Frankly," Dick explains, "when you have lots of people just creating these things for the sake of it, it does create noise. And it does also end up creating misinformation."

The problem is compounded by the trust that viewers instinctively place in facts and figures presented with the legitimizing veneer of authoritative fonts and crisp template layouts.[5] "At a certain point, you can convince people that they know more than they do," says Cezzar. "Many of these infographics make us feel like we understand things that we don't... These things are often not so easy to grasp. [When] we don't know anything about how that information is gathered, or what its limitations are, we don't have the capacity to understand."

This may appear like a new chapter in infographic history—one where incorrect data can be seen by millions. But Rendgen argues that botched diagrams have always been commonplace—the only real difference now is the scale and readership. As far back as 1914, so many misleading infographics were being published that a "how-to" book on creating accurate infographics was published, Willard Brinton's *Graphic Methods For Presenting Facts*. "Unfortunately," Brinton wrote in the book's preface, "there are extremely few draftsmen who know how to plot a curve or prepare any kind of a chart from data presented to them in the form of tabulated figures."

Rendgen explains that every time the field of infographics evolves, people pile into it quickly—but the expertise doesn't grow accordingly. "The democratization of infographics means that everybody can make one, but not everybody understands that you must bring some understanding of numbers and mathematical processing to make it work," she says. She is hopeful that in this Instagram iteration, like in others, creators will eventually catch up. Cezzar echoes this. She believes that data citations in viral infographics will become more common, in line with the improvements that historically happen over time.[6]

Though an Instagram infographic unpacking the meaning of "toxic positivity" may feel like a far cry from charting how to contain tuberculosis, the most important thing to remember as a consumer of infographics is that they are built to make an argument—regardless of what the issue might be. "It doesn't matter how you try," Dick says, "you can't switch off the argument."

(4)   Similarly, the graphic design platform Canva has had a big hand in defining the appearance of the current wave of infographics. In its 2020 end of year report, the site boasted that over 330,000 Black Lives Matter and Juneteenth templates were downloaded, which the site made available for free.

(5)   We also process information far more effectively when it is presented in a picture; according to research by the company that makes Post-it notes, visuals are processed 60,000 times faster than text.

(6)   It seems that viewers are becoming more savvy when it comes to what they expect from brands. Accounts such as @dietprada frequently call brands to account when they post about allyship without real-world action.

At Work With:
ORIOR

Brian Ng meets
the Irish family making New
York's favorite furniture.

Photography
ALEX WOLFE

> " You might think Irish design is *diddly, diddly, diddly.* You don't necessarily think *attitude.*"

Orior has always been a family business, but it was the pandemic that really brought it all back home to Newry, Northern Ireland. Ciarán McGuigan, the furniture brand's creative director, had flown back from his base in New York in March 2020 to check out some prototypes at the factory. Katie Ann, his sister, who has her own fashion label, returned from London two days later. And then the world shut down.

It was "class" being back with the family, says Ciarán. "We appreciate it now because we aren't teenagers being little shits." The McGuigan family are lined up for our Zoom interview on one side of a dining table, Brian (their father) on the far left, followed by Ciarán, then Rosie (their mother) and Katie Ann. Their computer's webcam is too narrow to take in this family portrait, so Ciarán spins the computer throughout the interview to face whoever is speaking.

Their unexpected time together has led to all sorts of collaborations, he says, one of which is a handwoven rug collection, whose colors were inspired by their walks: the different blues of the locks on the river, the sky's pinks and reds at sunset. They've been testing out new digitally printed fabrics, as well as fabrics woven from Donegal yarn, and wallpapers. And they're looking at fresh ways to combine materials—marble, metal, leather, fabric, crystal. "You might think Irish design is *diddly, diddly, diddly,*" says Ciarán, conjuring a parochial picture. "You don't necessarily think *attitude.*"

But "attitude" radiates from the brand's creative output: Its campaign photos of deep, velvet chairs, sculptural marble tables and mid-century-inspired cabinets have the light and saturation seemingly turned up so that they glow in jewel tones. In the section of the Orior website that documents their clients, chic creative types gaze at the camera, lounging on the furniture.

The desire for this kind of design did not exist in Ireland when Brian and Rosie were growing up in the 1960s and '70s. There were more pressing concerns. It was a bleak period politically—a time of violent conflicts between Irish nationalists, who wanted the six counties governed by the United Kingdom to be returned to the Irish republic, and the unionists, who wanted to keep their British identity. There were few job prospects during the Troubles. Brian, who grew up on Orior Road in Newry, left school at 15 and started working as an upholsterer in a factory. Soon after, he met Rosie at a rugby club just over the border in Dundalk.

Six or so months after they met, the couple left for Copenhagen in search of work. He was 18, she had just turned 17. They worked in fast-food restaurants and in hotels, window-shopping during their free time. There was all "this kind of color,

(below)
Newry is a sizeable city, but surrounded by the natural beauty of the Mourne Mountains and the Ring of Gullion.

design, clean lines," Rosie recalls. Back in Ireland, everything was brown and gray; in Copenhagen, it was in technicolor—they would pick up or crawl under the furniture to see how it was made.

In 1979, when they had been in Copenhagen for almost three years, Brian felt the itch to go back to Newry and try his hand at making his own furniture, based on the Danish designs that had enthralled them. He set up Orior immediately, hiring his sister as a sewer, his brother to handle sales and the next-door neighbor he grew up with to help with reupholstery, which they did for local clients for most of the week to make ends meet. In the snippets of downtime he could find, Brian designed his own original pieces. "It allowed us to be more creative in a small way," Brian says. Brian and Rosie established a storefront in Belfast for their tiny product line, but things were slow to pick up. Rosie says that it was so bad in those first years that had they put the furniture outside and tried to give it away, no one would've taken it. "Not in a month of Sundays could I have done what Dad had done back in the day," Ciarán says. "I had no choice," Brian counters.

Working in Northern Ireland was dangerous: Brian recounts how one time, when he was moving some furniture with a van, British troops thought he was a paramilitary. It was also difficult to convince local manufacturers to supply smaller quantities to artisans, meaning Orior had to get materials from overseas. A large, naturally tanned bull hide from Scandinavia was made into Brian's first design, the Shanog sofa. They worked with Kvadrat, the famous Danish fabric maker, back when they could only afford to put in tiny orders. At a Danish furniture exhibition, Rosie remembers the Kvadrat representative telling her encouragingly: "18 meters from you, 18 meters from the man in Hong

Kong, 18 meters from somebody in Germany. It all goes into the one pot." One English trader, by contrast, told them that the minimum order size was a thousand meters.

It was a hard slog during the first few years, until they started to secure bigger wholesale clients including Selfridges and Liberty in London. In the '90s and '00s, the Irish economy boomed and "things were absolutely flying," says Ciarán. Then, in 2008, the phones stopped ringing. Ireland became the first country in the eurozone to enter into a recession. Brian held on to his workforce—just—reasoning that their makers were highly skilled and they wouldn't be able to get them back if they let them go.

In 2013, Ciarán was "catapulted" into the family business. He was in Newry, on break from university in the US, when Brian got sick. Ciarán finished most of the rest of his degree via online learning, all the while helming the brand as its creative director. When Brian was well again, Ciarán decided to change Orior's focus to the American market, moving to New York City at the end of 2014 and opening a studio in Williamsburg, Brooklyn, on a shoestring budget in May 2015. They won a commission to fully outfit Vice Media's Toronto offices, and word of mouth began to spread through the rich and fashionable of the East Coast.

Orior's showroom is now in Tribeca, "a natural next step," according to Ciarán. There will also be an Orior hotel, of sorts: a client retreat in Savannah, to be opened at the end of the year. But Ciarán maintains Orior will stick to a slow drip of new products each year: only two or three new designs, and an updated handful from Brian's archives, which counts over 200. "I don't want to oversaturate," he says. And the brand, despite its US market, will remain resolutely Irish. To that end, Orior is investing more in training domestically—many of Ireland's talented makers currently go overseas for opportunity.[1]

Ciarán and Katie Ann, while intending to stay in their adopted cities for the next few years, are both thinking about returning to Newry permanently. "We have our own passions," Katie Ann says of herself and her brother, "and we have Orior as the glue that holds us all together." The pandemic has shown the family that they can operate a global brand from their hometown, which has a population of fewer than 30,000 people. "It's important in life," Rosie says, "that if you believe in something, you stick with it."

(1) Around 30 to 40 of the staff have been with the company for as many years. Orior is now hiring across the board and has recently brought two female Irish returnees on board as upholsterers (traditionally, makers have been male in Ireland), and its first Danish maker too.

(below)   Alongside his design career, Ciarán is a former professional footballer who played for Dundalk in Ireland and Syrianska FC in Sweden.

(left)   The countryside of County Down has been an inspiration to the family during the pandemic; the colors influenced the design of the new rug collection.
(above)   An advantage of working in Northern Ireland is that the Orior team is able to visit the country's many quarries and source raw materials directly from them.

IN TE
STUDIO:

Words
NANA BIAMAH-OFOSU

DIÉBÉDO FRANCIS KÉRÉ

Photography
DANIEL FARÒ

It's been almost 20 years since Diébédo Francis Kéré's first building, a primary school for his hometown of Gando, in Burkina Faso, was completed. Since then, Kéré has become one of Africa's leading architects—his work, steeped in craft, tradition and cultural relevance, celebrates people and communities.

These qualities earned him the Aga Khan Award for Architecture in 2004. Kéré has since built a successful international practice, with his studio based in Berlin and projects around the world, from Burkina Faso to the United States. Besides the primary school in Gando, other notable projects include the Lycée Schorge secondary school, also in Burkina Faso, a campus building comprising nine modules arranged radially around a courtyard, built primarily in local laterite stone with a secondary facade in eucalyptus wood. His 2017 Serpentine Pavilion in London, which included a transparent overhanging roof canopy, was inspired by the great tree, a place for gathering in his hometown. Even within his larger projects like Benin's National Assembly, which broke ground in spring 2021, Kéré's concerns for cultural continuity and purity in materiality, construction and craft still hold firm. In addition to his practice, he is also a distinguished educator, currently a professor at the Technical University in Munich, Germany.

We speak over Zoom, connecting from London to Berlin. Over the course of our wide-ranging conversation, I learn that, for Kéré, architecture always comes back to three things: making, culture and community.

NANA BIAMAH-OFOSU: You have spoken about Gando as "the village that raised you." What are your earliest memories of architecture?

DIÉBÉDO FRANCIS KÉRÉ: My earliest memory of architecture is as a child in Gando, playing in the central compound space of our house, and how it seemed to come alive through our social interactions—like sitting in a circle around my grandmother in the evenings. There was a great sense of atmosphere, a feeling of enclosure and security created by her voice and our movements as we absorbed the stories she told. I also remember architecture as hard work, repairing buildings after the rainy season. Architecture was equally romantic and practical.

NBO: How did these early memories translate into the direction you took with your education in Germany, especially your final-year project, the primary school in Gando?[1]

DFK: I tell students to think about their graduating project simultaneously as their last academic project and their first real project. The thesis project is a defining one for many architects; and I am no different in the sense that many of the questions I am still investigating—like the relationship between contemporary construction methods and traditional building techniques or issues of climate and weather—can be found in that first project.

NBO: You're now working at a larger scale and on buildings of national importance. You have said that people need "buildings that enhance their creativity and push them to take their future into their own hands." Can you elaborate on the role of architecture for community and nation building?

DFK: I am interested in architecture as a collaborative effort. With a project like the National Assembly in Benin,

that collaboration involves facing a country and reckoning not only with history but also the future.[2] The civic scale of the project demands something more than making shelter, it is a symbol of a democratic future. The form of the building references the history of the democratic process in Africa, where the canopy of a tree or the central compound space provided a place for gathering and governance. It was important in this project to make reference to the country's precolonial history.

NBO: I've always been fascinated by the colonial legacies embedded in civic buildings of a certain era on the African continent. How do you work with such memories?

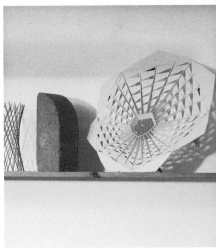

DFK: One of the significant damages of colonial power was its careless extraction of resources on the continent. In architecture, this was in the division between building and intellect—they came with the structures but didn't engage with the local culture, traditional building techniques or people. Therefore, architecture is still largely viewed as something for corporations, governments and institutions and nothing to do with the ordinary person. Jean Prouvé's Maison Tropicale, which now belongs to a museum, is an example of this problem. Had Prouvé involved the local people in his work, his buildings may have had a lasting legacy and impact on the African continent, an emotional connection beyond the image. I am interested in making architecture that resonates with local people.

---

(1)   Kéré's motivation to build a school for Gando was an acknowledgment of the relatively privileged position he was in growing up: As the son of the village chief, he was the only child within his cohort to go to school.

(2)   Alongside the National Assembly, Kéré designed a large public park: a symbol of democracy that encourages citizens to occupy the same space as politicians.

(below)   A model of a water tower for the Lycée Schorge secondary school in Palogo, Burkina Faso.
(right)   Kéré moved to Berlin shortly before the wall fell. He initially worked as a carpenter and went to night school for five years to finish his high school degree.

FEATURES

We are seeing a shift away from the Eurocentric worldview and toward Indigenous building traditions.

NBO: What methods do you use to ensure a collaborative approach, especially when working in a context where "proper" architectural drawings are limiting or poor tools for communication?

DFK: When working with a community like in Gando, it is about respecting their own specific cultural frame of reference. We also use 1:1 models to communicate on site—they feel more real. I find that drawings have their limitations—they are still fiction. If ideas on paper were the basis of making a better world, Africa, with all the supposedly visionary plans that people have developed for it, would be the most developed place on earth. We have to find other tools. Models are useful; they have a psychical presence, people can see them, touch them and understand them spatially.

NBO: You work a lot with earth as a building material. What's your approach to sustainability in your architecture?

DFK: I don't waste time talking about sustainability as fashion.[3] I am more interested in how it relates to a social economy, climatic conditions and people's ways of living. Sustainability is also about finding innovative ways of using materials. Take eucalyptus wood, for example, a fast-growing timber native to arid Burkina Faso, commonly used for scaffolding or firewood. We saw the ability to use it differently, as a proper building material, taking advantage of its durability. I am always thinking about sustainability, but as a practice that relates to context. A sustainable building is a durable building. It embraces its users and provides joy and comfort.

NBO: You emphasize the importance of utopianism in architecture, especially in times of crisis when we are implored to imagine beyond our present condition. What does that look like in practice?

DFK: That is a great summary of utopia and its usefulness in architecture; it is about the capacity to dream, to imagine a better and fairer world. Projects like the National Assembly in Benin are a manifestation of our utopian thinking. In our work, we apply this from the outset of a project—we ask how the particular project can push us in search of greater aspirations. You have to embrace a utopian vision to do things that are out of your reach.

NBO: People will often speak about an African architecture—do you think that such a thing exists?

DFK: It is dangerous to be limited. It is important to resist being reduced to pattern and form as an African architect. Pattern and form are of course part of architecture, but is it not the case that these differ from region to region on the continent? Architecture is best judged in place—for how it relates to climate, local resources, building techniques and its socioeconomic context. Of course, I believe in the architecture of the African continent—in an architecture that inspires people and gives a positive sense of our continent. The architecture of the African continent is simple, efficient and centers people.

(3) Kéré's approach to sustainability isn't one that prohibits the use of any particular method or material. He believes that factors such as using local materials and ensuring buildings cool themselves are equally important to consider.

Words
MICHELLE DEL REY

Cloistered behind ancient walls
and crammed with a catalog
of curios, an interior designer's
Santo Domingo home is an
autobiography writ from ruins.

Home Tour:
PATRICIA REID BAQUERO

The garden is ripe with pomegranates and pears. Orchids and ginger flowers are abundant. There's a pineapple centerpiece on the outdoor coffee table.

The house that this garden hems is interior designer Patricia Reid Baquero's private residence. It's a tropical oasis tucked inside Santo Domingo's Colonial Zone—the oldest part of the city, known colloquiallyas La Zona. In the morning, it hums with parrot songs.

As a child growing up in the Dominican capital, Reid Baquero adored strolling through the neighborhood with her mother, watching the domino players, bohemian artists and religious processions that dominated life at a street level. So when she found this property in 1980, she didn't hesitate. At that time, it was used as a multipurpose workshop rather than a home. "There were 50 or 60 people living here. It was in total ruins," Reid Baquero recalls. Along with her father, architect William Reid, and her brother, Carlos, Reid Baquero was determined to restore the residence to its 16th-century glory. The project ended up taking a decade: Reid Baquero only moved in in 1991 with her husband and their two daughters.

On approaching the house, arches outline the veranda and guide guests into the former carriage house that now functions as a formal living space. It is a room dominated by warm orange and beige hues and decorated with Reid Baquero's arrangements of saint figurines and clay pots, which she started gathering as a teenager.

The dining room is a space intended for family. The table was carved out of a saman tree that Reid Baquero's father planted following her birth. She uses it to host the family's Sunday dinners, per his request. For the first meal she ever served at the house, Reid Baquero remembers, she put together a decorative ensemble starring a Renaissance angel figurine and a string of lanterns to hover above her guests. The chairs are from her personal collection. Few of them match, but each tells a story. "When I moved into this house, I didn't buy a single piece of furniture or ornament because I was collecting all the time," she says.

Reid Baquero stumbled upon interior design by accident, having shown up to enroll at a nearby university and finding all the other programs full. She eventually landed scholarships to study museum design in Mexico and history of art and ethnic art in Spain—a background that elevates her

Photography
VICTOR STONEM

designs today. She's filled her home with trinkets and knickknacks, relying on flea markets and trips abroad to score new treasures. Sitars from Pakistan and architectural prints from England grace the walls. Some pieces are broken or faded, but Reid Baquero doesn't intend on changing them. "Beaucoup de caractère," she says.

Since establishing her interior design firm in 1973, Reid Baquero has worked locally and abroad. Some of her past clients include the singer Julio Iglesias and the late Dominican fashion designer Oscar de la Renta. De la Renta was a close family friend, says Reid Baquero, and a great admirer of her home. "A lot of people used to come to this house because Oscar told them that they should," she says. Reid Baquero takes a casual approach to curating her own home, but likes to stick to the brief while working with clients. Still, she always tries to put her stamp on projects, often with statues or antique chairs.

When the opportunity presented itself, Reid Baquero bought the house next door and combined the two properties. The old wall that divided the plots was altered and is now a gateway. She built a pool for her daughters and transformed the kitchen—pocked with old pigeonholes—into a barbecue area. She wonders about the future generations that might come visit the property. "I don't feel like I own it. I feel like I'm taking care of it," she says.

The neighborhood encompassing the Colonial Zone dates back to 1496, when the city was established by Christopher Columbus' brother Bartholomew. That's partly why Reid Baquero is hesitant to paint the over 500-year-old walls. When she added new structures during construction, she insisted on making them modern, so it would be easier to differentiate between the architectural styles. The area has seen a revival recently: New neighbors are moving in and developers are looking to make their mark. She doesn't mind, as long as the old buildings remain intact. "I think this city should be lived in," she says. "I don't want it to become a museum city."

Reid Baquero derived much of her eclectic style from her now-deceased parents, she says. In every corner of the house, she is reminded of her father, in particular. There is an area of the lawn, where two trees tower over the property in almost equal height, that's sentimental to her. Reid Baquero often stares at them, stretching toward the sky, imagining that, even now, they're connecting her to him.

" I think this city should be lived in.
I don't want it to become a museum."

(above)   Because it sits close to the equator, the Dominican Republic is warm and often rainy, creating perfect conditions for a tropical garden.
(right)   The home's eclectic collection includes Christian iconography, classical statues and Chinese ceramics.

迎客松

作於瓷都景德鎮

(left)
The formal living room at
Reid Baquero's Santo Domingo home.

101

Mediterranean
moments, handed to
you on a plate.

102   TABLE READ

Ceramics
LAURENCE LEENAERT
& LRNCE STUDIO
Photography
CHRISTIAN
MØLLER ANDERSEN

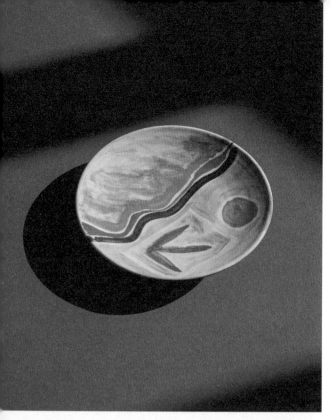

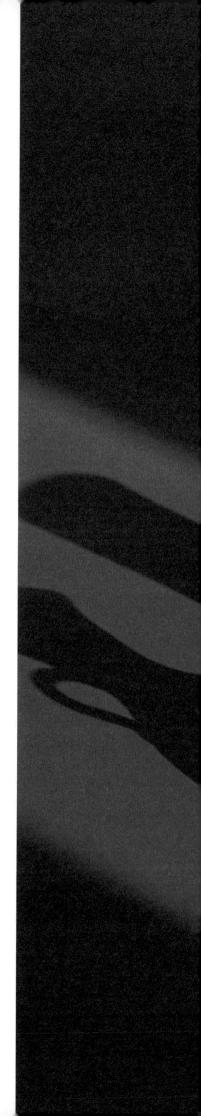

(above)   A vase and pitcher designed for *Kinfolk* by LRNCE, the Morocco-based studio founded by Belgian textile designer Laurence Leenaert.
(left)   Leenaert took inspiration from the beach to create the patterns that feature on this necked vase and plate.

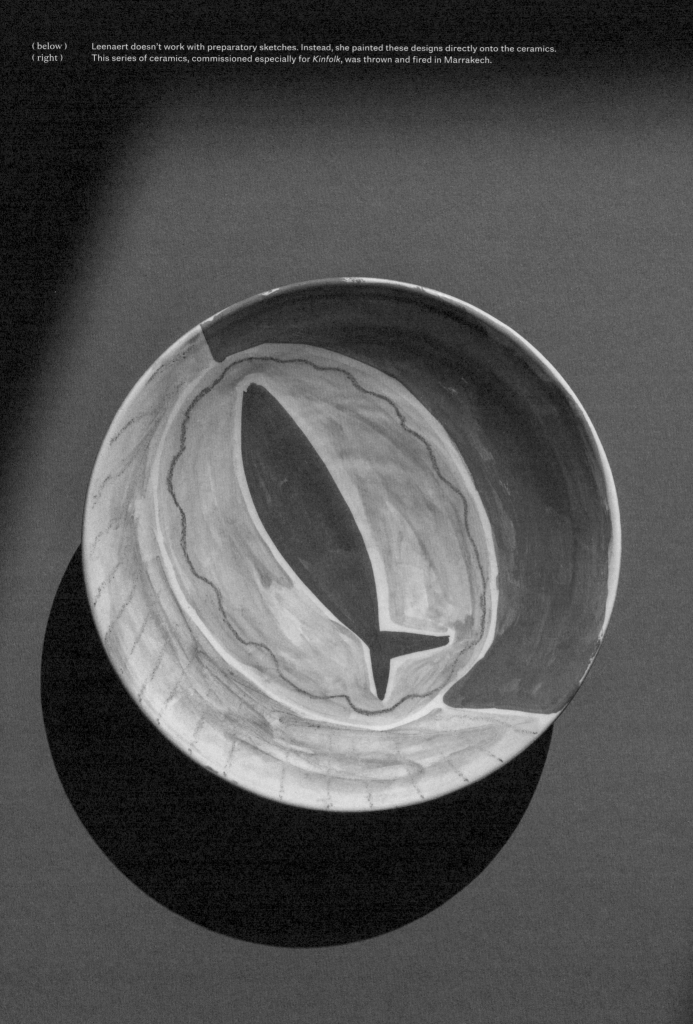

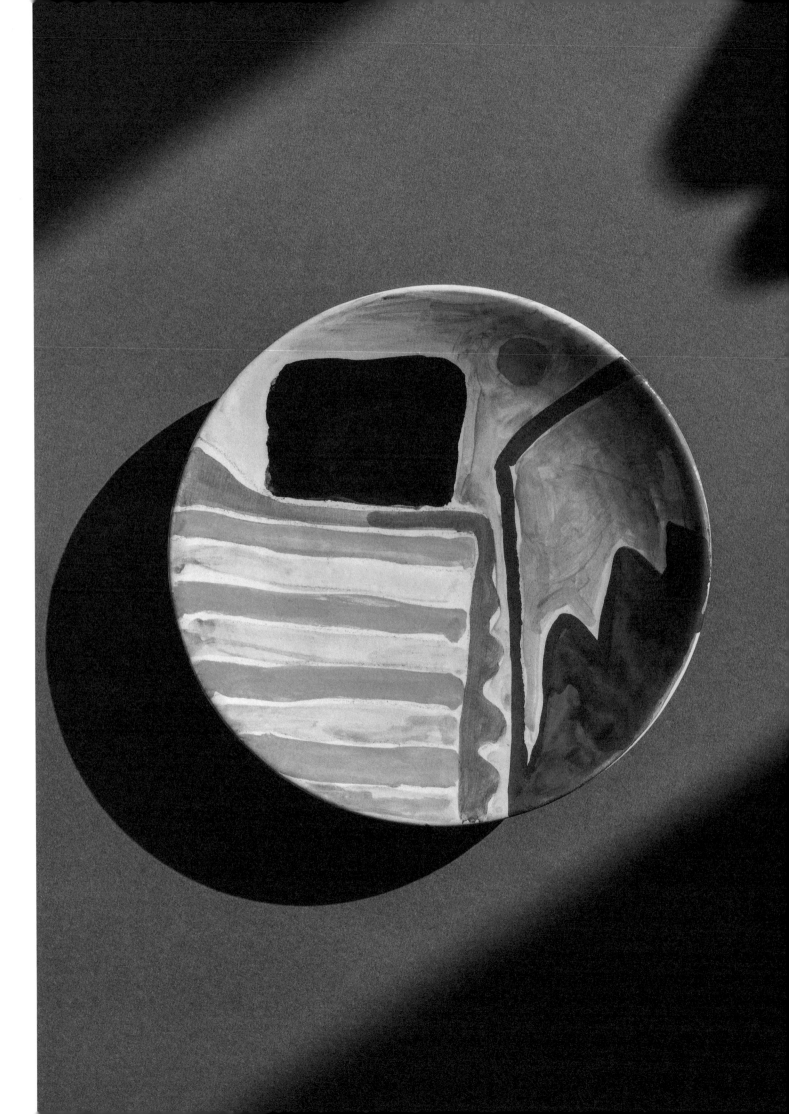

In an excerpt from our new book, Kinfolk Travel, winemaker Maher Harb takes us on a tour from grape to glass at his mountainside vineyard.

Extract:
IN THE VINEYARDS OF LEBANON

Words
LINA MOUNZER

Photography
BACHAR SROUR

Sept Winery lies high above the historic Lebanese coastal town of Batroun, at the end of a winding mountain road flanked by oak trees on one side and panoramic views over green valleys on the other. The air up there is crisp, a little dry, redolent with the smells of wild aromatic herbs—thyme, sage, oregano—and alive with the chirping of birds and crickets. The setting offers perfect conditions for Maher Harb, the owner of Sept, Lebanon's only biodynamic winery, to nurture the native grapes that he uses to make natural wines.

Harb is especially passionate about his mission: to highlight the value and singularity of what Lebanese vineyards have to offer. And he's not the only local winemaker who believes in the potential of this terroir. This, after all, is one of the oldest winemaking regions of the world, and tiny Lebanon boasts some fifty-six wineries. The number is made more impressive by the fact that after the end of the country's fifteen-year civil war in 1990, there were just five. Most are in the high-altitude plains of the Bekaa Valley, where a trip to Château Ksara (Lebanon's oldest and largest winery, founded in 1857 by Jesuit monks) or the newer Château Marsyas can be combined with a visit to the Roman ruins of Baalbek, which include a massive temple dedicated to Bacchus, the god of wine.

But Lebanon's winemaking is even older than the Romans; historical evidence shows that the Phoenicians were exporting wine to Egypt as early as 2,500 B.C., undoubtedly made with Lebanon's native grape varieties. It is these varieties that Lebanon's modern boutique wineries are trying to repopularize. While most of the older wineries use primarily French grapes, such as Cabernet Sauvignon, Merlot, and Cinsault, newer ones are using Lebanon's indigenous white varieties, such as creamy obeideh and citrussy merwah. Vintners such as Château Kefraya's Fabrice Guiberteau are going further and trying to reintegrate the indigenous red varieties, such as aswaad karech and asmi noir, that have fallen out of use.

(below)
Meadow flowers are grown alongside and among the vines at Sept. The edible ones make their way into dishes served on the terrace.

For such a small country, Lebanon's wines have impressive range as well as reach: many are available at boutiques or via online sales across the world. Connoisseurs interested in sampling them would do well to use wine writer Michel Karam's book *Wines of Lebanon* as a purchasing guide. But nothing beats a personal visit to a winery, where one can taste the wine while relaxing on the very terroir that gave it life. Better yet is to get a guided tour of the entire winemaking process from grape to glass, such as the one Maher Harb gives at Sept Winery.

Visit Sept—the best way to do so from Beirut is to rent a car or hire a private taxi—and you are visiting Harb's home, experiencing the same hospitality he would offer any personal guest. He will show you around, taking you across the terraced fields and into the dappled sunshine beneath the vines, explaining how they were grown. If you are hungry, he will cook for you: fresh, seasonal Mediterranean food "with a Lebanese twist." Often the fare includes what he has foraged from around the vineyard: wild asparagus and leeks, tender shoots of new garlic. He will spread the feast out on a wooden table beneath the open sky on a grassy ridge that overlooks an unmistakably Mediterranean vista: green hills cascading down through wisps of cloud toward the sea glittering at the very edge of the horizon. Various wines and vintages are of course carefully selected to pair with the food. He wants those who taste his wines to come away having tasted "his mountain, his Lebanon, his terroir."

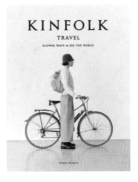

(above)
This story is an exclusive excerpt from our forthcoming book, *Kinfolk Travel*. Pre-order at Kinfolk.com now, or shop in stores worldwide from November.

Sept is Harb's passion project, more a calling than a business. This is something many businessmen say to personalize whatever brand they're selling, but in Harb's case, the philosophy by which he runs his vineyard is the one by which he conducts his life. He abandoned a lucrative but soulless career in France to come back and farm the fields that his father, who was killed during Lebanon's civil war, had left him.

Coming back to the land was a healing process for him, and, in turn, he practices the sort of farming that is a healing process for the land. Like all biodynamic vintners, he farms according to the lunar calendar, aiming to understand the earth's rhythms rather than employing chemicals to hurry them along to his own schedule. He uses no pesticides on the vines and no additives in the wine, making it natural.

Lebanon has been going through fraught times of late. The brief hope of an uprising in October 2019 gave way to an economic collapse that was exacerbated by the coronavirus pandemic. The currency went into freefall and many were left struggling to make ends meet. Then, in August 2020, over 2,000 tons (1,814 metric tons) of neglected ammonium nitrate ignited at the Beirut Port, resulting in one of the largest non-nuclear explosions in history. Harb, like so many Lebanese people, has been dizzied by every one of these blows, fighting to recover and readjust.

But throughout it all, he has kept the winery running, guided as ever by the rhythms of the planetary and lunar calendars that dictate the days on which to sow and which to reap. Like the land, it is constantly evolving.

And up there on his terraced fields, it isn't difficult to believe that the powerful force that commands the tides can exert the same magnetism on the nectar encased in the delicate skin of every grape. And it isn't difficult to feel, either, that everything that seems so overwhelming and insurmountable now in terms of the country's circumstances is just a brief turbulence across the face of this land's deep history. It has seen upheavals ranging from the rise and fall of empires—Phoenician, Roman, Ottoman—to earthquakes that wiped out entire cities and redrew the coastline. Nature's cyclical lesson becomes tangible when visiting Lebanon: that everything is eventually transmuted by time into the mulch of history, all of it feeding the richness of the terroir that Harb hopes can be tasted in every bottle of wine.

"Lebanon's winemaking is even older than the Romans."

113 — 176

Italian Cowboys, P.116
P.142 Search & Rescue,
The Beirut Lighthouse, P.146
P.150 A Three-Course Meal,
Moroccan Cinema P.170

THE COWBOYS OF TUSCANY.

In Italy's unruly Maremma,
a handful of horsemen corral cattle
at breakneck speeds.
Words LAURA RYSMAN
Photos ANDY MASSACCESI

In the southernmost stretch of Tuscany, known as the Maremma, wilderness still reigns. Beyond the manicured columns of cypress trees and pristine Renaissance villas that constitute the international image of this region, civilization exists in isolated clusters—the woodlands and marshes between them intimidatingly dense, and long considered inhospitable for all but the most tenacious souls. Where the wilderness meets the sea, rugged grasslands nourish the native Maremmana breed of broad-chested, lyre-horned cows, a species today protected by law, and guarded, in a tradition dating back to the ancient agriculture of the Etruscans, by Maremma's own cowboys—the handful of working horsemen known as *butteri*.

"Tradition keeps this work alive," says Stefano Pavin, head *buttero* at the Tenuta di Alberese, one of the few farms still employing the Maremman cowboys. "But very few people are cut out to be butteri today." He explains, "The animals are more important than you. You have to love it as a way of life—you can't think of it as work—or else it'll be too hard."

Pavin is acquainted with hard work. Before seven in the morning he mounts his Maremmano horse, riding at a full gallop out in the open fields for five hours, six days a week. There is no respite for holidays, rain or freezing cold. Dispersed across the 10,500 acres of Tenuta di Alberese, a primal terrain dotted with medieval watchtowers and umbrella pines, there are 400 Maremmana cows and 40 horses to be inspected and herded daily by Pavin and the three other men in his buttero contingent. The cowboys recognize each of the animals as effortlessly as the rest of us recognize our human friends. "We see them every day," says Pavin.

The butteri corral the cattle droves to their daily grazing pastures. Each spring, they tag newborns and break in untamed horses—rough, fast-moving tasks that inevitably topple a rider from the saddle once in a while.

Pavin stands crooked like a tree grown on windy terrain. Now 55, he's broken three ribs and a knee in his 34 years working as a buttero. His cartilage has been worn down along the length of his spine, and the last couple of years have turned his sandy hair a sun-bleached gray. Still, he says he'd like to keep riding well past the customary retirement age now looming on his horizon.

"I don't find our lifestyle difficult," Pavin says with a slanting smile. "Especially after this year when everyone was locked up in their apartments, and we were out in the fields on our horses every day. [We are] the luckiest people in the world."

The Maremmano horses that Pavin and the other butteri ride are a tall, indigenous breed the color of molasses, with robust legs to carry them through the thorny, swampy brush, and a wide barrel of a body that bows the cowboys' legs in a permanent arch. In a small barn pungent with the smell of rawhide, the butteri keep dozens of Maremmana saddles, each stitched like oversized baseball mitts and padded inside with horsehair to cushion riders on their long shifts. On the barn walls dangle tarred lengths of rope for controlling calves, and the cowboys' hooked *uncino* staffs carved from dogwood. Leather gaiters and waxed cotton rain jackets hang in a corner, custommade by area artisans and, in some cases, mothers of butteri.

The handcrafted gear is a testament to a heritage painstakingly sustained. The European Union funds a course to cultivate the next generation of modern butteri. (A changing demographic: Of the last cohort's eleven students, nine were women.)[1] The region of Tuscany took over operations at Tenuta di Alberese in 1979, in order to ensure the survival of the tradition. The massive cows, which can grow past 2,500 pounds, once served as beasts of burden; since the advent of farm machinery, the cattle have been raised for organic beef, but they roam these vast Maremman pastures freely and until late in their years.

Tenuta di Alberese also invites the public in—it's the only place where visitors have the opportunity to ride through the fields with butteri, but Pavin warns: "Tourists have to be ready to adapt to the demands of our work." So: Show up at 6:30 a.m., gallop until lunchtime. It doesn't matter that your legs are aching. The animals are more important than you.

Where the iconic American cowboy is an agent of conquest, the buttero of Maremma is the guardian of these Tuscan creatures and the natural expanses vital for them to remain semiwild. It's an arduous but plainly rewarding existence for those who prefer the arcadian landscape, with all its vicissitudes, to the common comforts of the city.

"It's not easy to be happy in life—arriving at a sense of balance is always a problem," says Pavin, his blue eyes contemplating the distance. "But there are moments out there when I'm alone and witnessing this marvel of nature and I find myself at peace with everything."

(1) The Tuscan regional government's two-month vocational training course, "Rediscovering the Buttero," was inaugurated in 2019. It was the first time that women were actively encouraged to train for the demanding role.

"You have to love it as a way of life. You can't think of it as work, or else it'll be too hard."

(previous)   Despite the vaunted position of Tuscany in the popular imagination, the Maremma remains one of the least visited regions of Italy.
(left)   The regional park where the butteri work is built on reclaimed marshland. The region is so rural because, for centuries, it was uninhabitable.

(left)
Much of the Maremma is dotted with umbrella
pines, whose distinctive silhouette is common to
several Mediterranean countries.

(right)   The butteri use an *uncino* to herd cattle. The long, thin stick is also used to close gates without dismounting.
(overleaf)   The Maremma bulls have long and open lyre-shaped horns, while the cows have crescent-shaped horns.

"I don't find our lifestyle difficult. Especially after this

year when everyone was locked up in their apartments."

Dora Dalila Cheffi is building her reputation, and her home, in the Tunisian capital.
Words LAYLI FOROUDI Photos YOANN CIMIER

AN ÆRTIST IN TUNIS.

Dora Dalila Cheffi sees her art—whether painting, filmmaking or sculpting—as learning. The Finnish-Tunisian artist grew up in Helsinki, and only knew Tunisia through childhood summer visits to her father's side of the family in Sfax, an industrial port town. In 2018, at the age of 28, she relocated to Tunis after graduating from art school. She wanted to connect with her father's country—although he himself wasn't initially thrilled with the decision, as he didn't see Tunisia as a place with many opportunities for success.

But Cheffi has flourished here. As part of her artistic exploration, she hybridizes and inverts traditional materials and aesthetics, reinterpreting Tunisian scenes in wild colors in her paintings, and drawing on the heritage of Sejnane pottery in her ceramic creations.

We speak at her studio off a gravel road in Bhar Lazreg, a quiet working-class neighborhood in the north of Tunis, while eating a breakfast of apricots and melon cubes and bread dipped in ricotta and olive oil. There is a big painting on one wall and a bright green suit, that she plans to film a friend dancing in, hanging on the other; both will feature in her solo exhibition at local contemporary art gallery B7L9 in early 2022.

LAYLI FOROUDI: This table spread looks like it might be the subject of one of your paintings.

DORA DALILA CHEFFI: Breakfast is my favorite time of the day. I'll have a shit day if I rush it. And aesthetically, it's cute because you have all these different colors and plates and little things—melon slices can become weird shapes, and then you have the olives that have reds and greens. But maybe the whole breakfast thing started because I had breakfast and then I went to my studio. And I was like, *Well, I just had breakfast, maybe I'll paint that.*

(above)   Cheffi's studio is in the experimental art space B7L9, where she will present a solo show next year.

(left)
Cheffi's kitchen, with one of her many
food-themed paintings hanging on the wall.

LF: That would have begun around the time you were settling into Tunis. Was it partly about feeling at home?

DDC: Yeah absolutely. The food series was just me taking what I felt to be familiar at the time and what I could relate to. Now I've been here for a while and breakfast is part of my life, but it's like when you walk down the same road every day, you don't see it in the same way anymore. That's why, for me, I get annoyed that everyone kept wanting to see more breakfast and breakfast and breakfast. It's important to move forward.

LF: What are the things you moved on to, or want to move on to?

DDC: Well the first series was about sceneries, it was about naively painting things and buildings that I was seeing; kind of things I was missing. Then, I started painting more people because I had made friends but there were also the more awkward feelings that come with a place when the honeymoon phase is over.

LF: You worked more in photography and ceramics before. Did you come to Tunis wanting to paint?

DDC: I just wanted to connect here, without my family, on my own. I had the idea of doing a documentary project about the "third culture kid" thing. I interviewed people, like a guy I bumped into, who had Tunisian roots but spoke broken Arabic. He was getting all emotional because he could now understand the lyrics of the Tunisian song "Nghir Alik" by Ÿuma.

LF: Do you have a song or something that provokes a similar emotion?

DDC: I would always hear a lot of mezoued songs growing up. When I first moved to Tunisia, people told me I would use really weird words and phrases [when speaking Arabic], and it's because I learned them from these songs—sad songs that people listen to when they get drunk. They're all about crying and sadness and heartbreak. My dad thinks they're rubbish, and too emotional.

LF: Tell me about your upcoming exhibition.

DDC: The working title is "3okba lik" which is a phrase you hear a lot. It's a good thing to say, like to wish you success for your studies, but then after studies it becomes about marriage;

"God willing you'll get married and get this happiness." It's meant well but I'm like, What if that's not the happiness I want?

LF: This painting on the wall looks quite bright and happy.

DDC: This was [painted from] a pregnancy shoot with my friend, which was fun. In Beyoncé's pregnancy shoot she was like the Virgin Mary, but unmarried women are not viewed like that. So I said, Let's make you like that and celebrate this way of bringing a child into the world. Visually, weddings are loud and obnoxious in a way I find cool. I want my exhibition to look like an obnoxious wedding reception.

LF: Do you think Tunis has shaped the style of your work?

DDC: I don't think it would have been the same if I had stayed in Finland. Tunisia really has a special light. Everything looks so rich. But, here, a lot of artists make dark or black-and-white stuff. Whereas in Finland, a lot of artists make very colorful bold works even though Finland is so gray and cold. It's almost like the grass is always greener on the other side.

"Tunisia really has a special light."

(BALEARICS)

TILE
MAKING
IN
MALLORCA.

Biel Huguet charts the history of his island in colorful cement.
Words BAYA SIMONS
Photos MARINA DENISOVA

THE MEDITERRANEAN

It was the 1992 Olympics in Barcelona that changed the fate of Mallorca, the Balearic island off the coast of Spain. In the decades leading up to the Olympics, the once sleepy island—a midpoint between Europe and North Africa—had been shocked awake by a mass influx of British vacationers in search of cheap sunshine. The surge of tourism had led to the destruction of traditional Mallorcan architecture to make way for modern hotels and holiday homes.[1]

But Barcelona's Olympic tourists were different, keen to discover the cultural charms of Catalonia: its Moorish architecture, distinctive cuisine and the fantastical, omnipresent influence of Gaudí. All these interests eventually pointed visitors toward Mallorca, the nearest island to the city. "They wanted a kind of Tuscany," recalls Biel Huguet, director of tile manufacturer Huguet. "They said, 'I want a house, but I don't want this rubbish you built in the '80s or '90s. I want traditional materials. I want a Mediterranean house.'"

The rise and fall and rise again of Huguet follows the island's wider trajectory. The company was founded by Biel's grandfather in 1933, producing cement tiles using the traditional hydraulic method, in which colored liquid cement is extruded into a mold. Huguet was part of a lineage of Catalan craftspeople who have made tiling using this technique—favored for its ability to hold intricate patterns while remaining durable—since the 1850s. The history actually extends back thousands of years to the hot climes of ancient Egypt, where the material first became popular for interior surfaces (rather than roofs) due to its cooling effect. "There was a big tradition of producing this kind of architecture, or the elements of architecture, in Mallorca. We have very deep roots that go back to the Romans, to Arabic culture and to Catalan," says Biel. Tile making, he believes, is quintessentially Mediterranean. "The weather, the sun, the light, the colors, the materials and the lifestyle have adapted, over years, to all these issues."

In the 1960s, the craft came under threat. Biel's father, a well-known Catalan poet who was running the business at the time, stopped producing traditional tiles and pivoted the business toward the cement beams and blocks that were in high demand for the hotels and villas popping up all over the island. "There were around 100 factories like ours," Biel says of the years before the tourism boom. "Each village was producing their own tiles because there were no roads between most of the villages in Mallorca. And from the '60s to the '80s, all of them

disappeared or changed. Just a single man in a little village was producing tiles in the '90s. Nothing had changed in 700 years, and then it changed in 20." When Biel took over the company in 1997, he set out to recover its traditional origins. "I thought, I will focus on traditional architecture and on a local market," he says.

He began to see the possibilities of applying the traditional technique of tile making to contemporary design. Now, the company is the go-to for cement tiles, in demand for both their contemporary designs—milky pastel tones, chunky geometric patterns—and traditional tiling in bolder colors and intricate patterns. Huguet has cleverly tapped into the Instagram-led appetite for behind-the-scenes videos of satisfying production processes; the clips posted to its account of creamy lemon-colored cement being poured into sharp geometric molds rack up tens of thousands of views.

It has also become the collaborator of choice for some of the biggest architects working today. Pritzker Prize–winning Swiss firm Herzog & de Meuron often use Huguet's triangular tiles to give floors and walls the simultaneously otherworldly and ancient appearance of cracked earth, while English architect David Chipperfield commissioned the company to make bespoke terrazzo column plinths and wall claddings for his redesign of Selfridges, London's iconic department store. Architects and designers come to Huguet, Biel says, because they have continued using their storied traditional technique while keeping the designs fresh. "People are not interested in my grandmother's style," he says. "The technique is very interesting, the roots, the background, the history, the craft, that's very important. But we need to update it technically and aesthetically."

For Huguet, the challenge is to continue innovating and adapting their aesthetic, in order to keep the craft alive, but more importantly, as a way of defining what it means to be Mallorcan in the 21st century. "Otherwise, everything is Ikea. We have something that has roots and identity. So we have to share it with the world. I think that this is a way for us to survive. And also for the world to be a little bit richer, culturally and architecturally."

(1) Mass tourism remains a concern in Mallorca. In 2017, planes passed through Palma de Mallorca airport at a rate of one every 90 seconds; in 2019, 11.8 million visitors flooded the island, dwarfing the local population of under a million and skyrocketing the cost of living.

(right)
Biel Huguet is part of the third
generation running the Huguet family business.

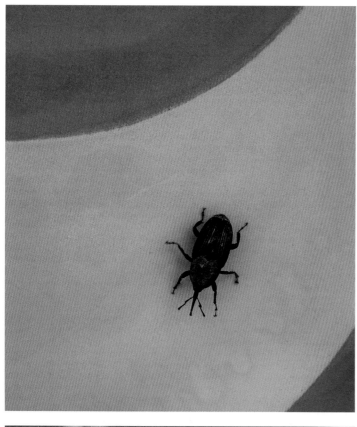

(above)   An assortment of colorful tiles from Huguet's collaboration with Spanish architect Carme Pinós.
(right)   The Huguet factory has been based in the small rural town of Campos in the southeast of Mallorca since 1933.

"Nothing had changed in
700 years, and then it changed in 20."

Olivia Spili, of the NGO Sea-Watch, details
a very different Mediterranean reality.
Words STEPHANIE D'ARC TAYLOR

(EUROPE)

A DESPERAE CROSSING.

Left Photograph: Laila Sieber. Previous Photograph: Martina Bjorn

"The departures are not decreasing, as we hear from politicians."

During the last decade, the Mediterranean has become a route to Europe for people from all over the world looking for a better life. Libya and Tunisia are staging points for sea crossings, where vulnerable people are subject to horrific abuse, exploitation and torture by both the authorities and those who take their money to facilitate the journey. Europe and the rest of the world have turned a blind eye to the over 20,000 people who are officially recorded as having died in the Mediterranean since 2014. The true figure may be much higher.

The German NGO Sea-Watch has stubbornly held a finger in the dam of scandalous indifference. Since its founding in 2014, its ships have rescued more than 38,000 people from boats ill-equipped for the crossing. Olivia Spili is a protection officer for Sea-Watch and has been aboard its ships for three rescue missions.

STEPHANIE D'ARC TAYLOR: How have things changed in the Mediterranean since your first mission?

OLIVIA SPILI: The rhythm of rescues is very different now. On my first mission, we had one rescue and 65 people on board. On my last mission we had six rescues in 72 hours, and 466 people on board.

SDT: Is the migrant crisis being accurately represented in the media?

OS: The departures are not decreasing, as we hear from politicians. I think we've already had something like 27,000 people arriving in Europe [between January and June 2021]. But the problem with the numbers is that we can register the arrivals, but there's no way of knowing how many departures there are from the Libyan and Tunisian coasts. That's the big question mark. According to the International Organization for Migration, so far this year 773 people have been declared dead or missing in the Mediterranean. Last year there were 290. So it's already three times more than what it was last year. There's no transparency or clarity to these numbers. And this is the way institutions want it to be; they have no interest in knowing the real numbers.

SDT: What is the most common misperception?

OS: The idea that this journey is an easy one. People in Europe think that people in Africa just decide to take a boat trip. That's not what is happening out there. The people I spoke to wait an average of four to six years before actually making it onto a boat. There is violence and torture and kidnapping and ransoms. Also, it's scary out there. On my first mission, we couldn't find a boat for hours. I remember this feeling of being so small in the middle of the sea. And I was on a safe boat with a GPS tracker so I could never get lost. It's crazy how a little wave can be so big that you don't see the horizon anymore. A bit of fog and then you're lost. I don't think a mother would risk the life of a child if it was not her last choice.

SDT: What is the most uncertain moment in a rescue?

OS: There's one moment in every rescue: On my first mission, when we saw the boat, I was like, *What am I going to say? How can I make them trust me and follow my instructions?* If they start jumping because they're happy, that could capsize the boat. You need them to trust and listen to you. It's never over until it's really over and everyone is safe on the ship.

SDT: What are some of the moments of connection that have affected you the most?

OS: My second and third missions we had hundreds of people. But on my first mission we had only 65 people and we stayed with them for eight days. So we got to know each other one on one. I remember one man was telling me what he'd been through in Libya. And then at one point, he said, "I will stop there because I don't want to hurt you." I thought, *We've known each other for only three days. How is it that you care about not hurting me, when it's you who went through hell?*

SDT: What's the hardest part of the missions for you?

OS: The most difficult part is the disembarkation. I know that on board the ship we listen to people's stories, we treat them, there are doctors, there's food. But on land, this will most likely not be the same. The most frequent question I get on disembarkation is, "Do you think I'll be able to go to school?" And you have to let people go into a world that you know is nothing like what they're imagining. Most won't get asylum because the system doesn't work. Most will be sent back home or will maybe have to live in Europe undocumented and that's not a life you wish for anyone. So watching people get off the ship is the hardest part, knowing that they most likely will be hurt again and their expectations won't be met.

SDT: What keeps you coming back to volunteer with Sea-Watch?

OS: On the last mission, when we were disembarking people in Sicily, one man thanked me for treating him like a human being. The fact that a grown man has to say thank you for treating him like a human being means there is something systematically wrong. This is why we do it. I don't know if what we do at Sea-Watch is the solution, but I want to believe that it's part of it.

(1) Spili's last mission was aboard the NGO's Sea-Watch 4 ship. In its first mission, Sea-Watch 4 rescued over 350 people from distress at sea and brought them to safety.

(left) Olivia Spili, who, as a protection officer for Sea-Watch, has taken part in three search and rescue missions in the Mediterranean. While the stories in this section present an idealized portrait of aspects of the Mediterranean, we feel it is important to not turn a blind eye to the terrible realities playing out along the same stretch of coastline.

Beirut's old *manara*, the Arabic word for lighthouse, is perched on a hill facing the sea. The neighborhood where this black-and-white striped 82-foot tower is located was even named after it. Victor Chebli, whose family have been lighthouse keepers in the country for over 150 years, is committed to shining a light on Lebanon's past. This lighthouse is not only a historic building but also a monument to the country's resilience and a reflection on how individuals are playing a leading role in preserving the city's heritage.

SABINA LLEWELLYN-DAVIES: Growing up in a lighthouse sounds like every kid's dream come true. What was it like for you?

VICTOR CHEBLI: I was born here. As you can see, our family living quarters are annexed to the lighthouse. Being situated on shore in Beirut, I never felt isolated, unlike lighthouse keepers out on islands. There was always so much going on here. But of course it was not always easy. I was called on to help with the chores such as carrying gallons of kerosene to fuel the light. That was tiring. Then, in 1952, a French ship, the Champollion, sank off the coast of Beirut. My father was accused of not lighting the beam and thus causing the sinking. I was just a toddler at the time. He was sent to jail but thankfully he was proven innocent and released three months later. That same year, France sent a team over to evaluate the lighthouse and they offered to build a more modern structure that we moved into in 1957.

SLD: Having just climbed almost 300 steps to the top myself, I'm sure it must have been exhausting operating the lighthouse before automation. How did day-to-day operations change in the 1950s?

VC: When we moved to the [newer] lighthouse we had new machinery and electricity; it was very advanced, maybe the most advanced lighthouse in the region. A lift was installed, so there was no need to carry equipment up the stairs anymore. Electricity powered the beam, so there was no need for kerosene fuel. Operations became a lot easier. What remained the same was that my father still had to get up early every day to switch off the light at sunrise and return at sunset to switch it on to guide ships ashore. And I still do that to this day, day in day out.

SLD: Did your father expect you to take over the keeping of the lighthouse from him?

VC: For more than 150 years, the Chebli family has been in charge of guiding ships to Beirut—ever since the first lighthouse structure was built during the Ottoman Empire in the late 19th century. So, yes it was expected. I took over in 1973 after my father retired.

SLD: Just after you became the lighthouse keeper, Lebanon entered into its 15-year civil war. Many thousands were displaced from Beirut. Was it tough to stay and maintain the lighthouse?

VC: The war began in 1975. They were difficult years. I was kidnapped three times and our living quarter was hit several times by gunfire and bombs. I had to keep the lighthouse dark at night for safety reasons until the ceasefire in 1990, but I used to light it up during the day just to keep the engines from rusting. We never abandoned it. I repaired our home as well as I could and we sheltered in the basement with our four children waiting for peace.

SLD: Did you ever wish to leave the lighthouse, leave Beirut, maybe even to emigrate to another country?

VC: Our family has been in Beirut for 200 years. Our home was severely damaged, as was the lighthouse, but we rebuilt it. This is where I was born and this is where I will die. Now, my sons Joseph and Raymond help me with the daily maintenance and when I retire they will take over.

SLD: At the age of 72, you may just be the oldest lighthouse keeper in the world. How does that make you feel?

VC: Really? Maybe. Well, I haven't really thought about it. I can't imagine doing anything else.

Victor Chebli has weathered storms,
war and three kidnappings to maintain his family's shining legacy.
Words SABINA LLEWELLYN-DAVIES
Photos BACHAR SROUR

(LEBANON)

THE LIGHTHOUSE KEEPER OF BEIRUT.

(left)   A Fresnel lens uses glass prisms to refract and reflect light into a single powerful beam.
(below)   The view from Beirut's old lighthouse to the sea has been blocked by newly constructed high-rise buildings.

(RECIPES)

A MEDITERRANEAN SUPPER.

Four citrusy recipes from the kitchen of *Anissa Helou.*
Words ANISSA HELOU
Photos LAUREN BAMFORD
Food Styling STEPHANIE STAMATIS

THE MEDITERRANEAN

ZA'LOUQ
Steamed Eggplant in a Tomato and Cilantro Sauce

You can also serve this delectable Moroccan salad as a vegetarian main course; simply double the quantities. I often vary the flavor by using parsley instead of cilantro.

1 pound eggplants (2 medium)
3 garlic cloves
1 (28-ounce) can Italian peeled plum tomatoes
1/3 cup extra-virgin olive oil
1 bunch fresh cilantro, most of the bottom stalks discarded, finely chopped
1/2 teaspoon ground cumin
Juice of 1/2 lemon, or to taste
1/4 teaspoon paprika
1/4 teaspoon dried chile flakes
Sea salt, to taste

Peel the eggplants lengthways, leaving thin strips of skin. Quarter them lengthways and slice across into pieces about ½ inch thick.

Steam the eggplant pieces and peeled garlic cloves for 30 minutes, or until very soft. While the vegetables are steaming, drain the tomatoes (reserve the juice for another use), discard the seeds, and chop them coarsely.

Put the oil in a sauté pan. Add the chopped tomatoes, cilantro and cumin and mix well. Cook over medium-high heat, stirring occasionally, for about 15 minutes or until the juices have evaporated and the sauce looks fresh and chunky.

When the eggplants and garlic are ready, mash them with a fork or a potato masher. (Don't use a food processor as the eggplants will become too mushy.)

Add the mashed eggplants and garlic to the tomato sauce together with the lemon juice, paprika, chile flakes and salt. Mix well and simmer over low heat for another 15 minutes, stirring regularly. It should have a soft but chunky texture. Taste and adjust the seasoning if necessary. Let cool and serve at room temperature.

L'HAM M'CHERMEL
Lamb Tagine with Olives and Preserved Lemons

Jemaa el Fna is the ultimate place for street food in Morocco and before it became the evening gathering place in Marrakech, it was a national bus terminal. As with all terminals, there was a large group of street vendors stationed there to cater to the multitude of travelers in need of nourishment or refreshment. When the bus station moved to its present location at Bab Doukkala, the vendors stayed behind in Jamaa el Fna and, eventually, it became a tourist attraction. It is great fun to walk around the square and watch the cooks serve the crowds. Tagine with olives and preserved lemons is always on the menu, but it's usually prepared with chicken. On the street, the chickens are boiled separately from the sauce and look as if

they have been dyed bright yellow (probably because of the turmeric added to the cooking water). The sauce is also much simpler and made without herbs. This version is what you would have in homes or in fancy restaurants.

1 garlic clove, finely chopped
1/2 teaspoon ground ginger
1/4 teaspoon cumin
1/4 teaspoon paprika
Pinch of saffron filaments, crushed
Sea salt and finely ground black pepper
4 lamb shanks (about 4 pounds in total)
2 medium onions, thinly sliced
1/2 bunch fresh flat-leaf parsley, most of the bottom stalks discarded, very finely chopped
1/2 bunch fresh cilantro, most of

the bottom stalks discarded, very finely chopped
1 cinnamon stick
2 tablespoons extra-virgin olive oil
2 tablespoons butter
Juice of 1/2 lemon, or to taste
1 large preserved lemon, peel only, cut lengthways into strips
1 cup green or purple olives

Combine the garlic, ground ginger, cumin, paprika, saffron, a little sea salt and 1/4 teaspoon pepper in a large Dutch oven.

Add the lamb shanks and rub well with the spice mixture. Add the onions, parsley and cilantro. Barely cover with water (about 5 cups) and add the cinnamon stick. Bring to a boil over

medium-high heat, then add the oil and butter. Cover and let simmer for 1 hour, or until the meat is cooked and the broth has become very concentrated.

Remove the shanks to a serving platter and keep warm. Discard the cinnamon stick. Reduce the heat to medium-low and simmer the sauce gently, covered, for a further 15 minutes, stirring regularly, until the onion has more or less disintegrated.

Add the lemon juice, preserved lemon peel and olives. Return the shanks to the pan, turning them in the sauce carefully. Simmer for a few more minutes. Taste the sauce and adjust the seasoning if necessary. Transfer the shanks to a serving platter. Pour the sauce all over and serve very hot with good bread.

KHIZU M'QALLIYA
Braised Saffron Carrots with Parsley

Good pinch of saffron filaments
1/4 cup extra-virgin olive oil
3 garlic cloves, finely chopped
1½ pounds baby carrots, peeled or
    scrubbed clean
1/4 bunch fresh flat-leaf parsley,
    most of the bottom stalks discarded,
    finely chopped
1/2 teaspoon finely ground black pepper
Sea salt, to taste

Soak the saffron in 1/2 cup water for 30 minutes.

In a medium saucepan, combine the rest of the ingredients. Add the saffron water and place over medium-high heat. Bring to a boil, then cook, covered, stirring occasionally, for 10 minutes or until the carrots are just tender and the sauce is reduced. Serve hot, warm or at room temperature.

QA'B EL-GH'ZAL
Cornes de Gazelles

Qa'b el-gh'zal, or cornes de gazelles, are rarely prepared at home. Instead they are bought from women who specialize in making them and other sweets, who will only make them to order. While in Marrakech one time, I found exquisite qa'b el-gh'zal in an unpromising-looking bakery. They were so good that I bought some every day to take to the café next door where I had them with my morning mint tea. The waiter disapproved of my breakfast, explaining that cornes de gazelles are normally served in the afternoon with tea, or offered at the end of fancy dinners (known as diffa). This recipe comes from the woman who made the pastries that I so enjoyed. However hard I try, I'm never able to roll the dough as thinly as hers to achieve her pastries' melting texture. Makes about 40.

FOR THE FILLING
5 cups blanched almonds
1½ cups confectioners' sugar
1/4 cup orange flower water
2 tablespoons unsalted butter, softened
½ teaspoon ground mastic (optional)

FOR THE PASTRY
2 cups all-purpose flour
2 tablespoons unsalted butter, melted, plus softened butter for working the pastry

To make the filling: Soak the almonds in boiling water for 15 to 20 minutes, then drain and dry well.

Put the almonds and confectioners' sugar in a food processor and process until very finely ground and kind of sticky, like a paste (you might have to do them in several batches). Transfer to a mixing bowl. Add the orange flower water, softened butter and ground mastic, if you are using it, and mix with your hands to a homogeneous paste. Cover the almond paste filling with a clean cloth and set aside.

To make the pastry: Preheat the oven to 400°F. Put the flour in a shallow mixing bowl and make a well in the middle. Add the melted butter to the well and gradually add 2/3 cup water, working it in with your fingers. Knead for a few minutes, or until the dough has a slightly looser consistency than that of bread.

Divide the almond paste into 40 pieces. Roll each into a ball and then into a small sausage about 4 inches long with tapering ends.

Smear your pastry board, rolling pin and hands with softened butter. Take a piece of dough and roll it out, turning it over once or twice, into a very thin strip about 4½ inches wide. Carefully stretch the dough with your hands to widen and thin it a little more, then place an almond paste sausage at one end, about ¾ inch away from the edge. Fold the dough tightly over the almond paste and pinch the filling upwards and sideways, bending it at the same time, to form a crescent with a thin triangular body. Press the edges of the dough together and cut, following the shape of the crescent, using a fluted pastry wheel. The crescent should measure about 4 inches long by 1¼ inches high. Prick with a fine needle in several places on both sides and place on a nonstick baking sheet, or one lined with parchment paper.

Repeat the process, using up the rest of the dough strips, until you have shaped the first 20 crescents. Bake for 10 minutes, or until they are barely colored.

While the first batch is baking, continue making the cornes de gazelle and bake as before. (You might have a little dough leftover, but you shouldn't have any filling left unused. If you do, it means that you haven't rolled out the dough thinly enough.) Let the pastries cool before serving. They will keep for at least a week in an airtight container.

AN HERB SHOP IN ATHENS.

Herb specialist *Evangelia Koutsovoulou*
treats Greek greens with the same reverence as wine and cheese.
Words SARAH SOULI Photos CHRIS KONTOS

"In villages, every old woman knows at least 10 wild greens growing nearby."

On a sun-drenched corner in the Neos Kosmos neighborhood of Athens, Evangelia Koutsovoulou has set up the office, laboratory and tasting room for Daphnis and Chloe, a herb company that has been capturing the heady aroma of Greece since 2013. Koutsovoulou, who is originally from central Greece, collaborates with organic farmers around the country, using sustainable farming practices to grow small quantities of indigenous herbs. Like many Greeks who live outside of big cities, Koutsovoulou grew up eating and drinking freshly foraged herbs such as wild thyme, oregano and mountain tea. But as she began traveling as a young adult, she realized that most people in Greek cities and elsewhere in Europe were cooking with old, mostly dried herbs.

The shop is a labor of both love and patience: Scattered across Greece's mountain ranges and its numerous islands are different kinds of terroirs, with hundreds of varied herbs. With dogged precision, Daphnis and Chloe highlights regional favorites (Cretan dittany, chili flakes from Almopia, Aegean oregano). On a quiet morning at the tail end of spring, Koutsovoulou spoke about the smell of Greek summer, the power of herbs and how to be a sustainable forager.

SARAH SOULI: Let's start with the senses. What's the first herb you remember?

EVANGELIA KOUTSOVOULOU: Definitely oregano, because as kids we would spend all our summers in the mountains, in a small house outside of a tiny village where oregano was growing on the side of the street. It's one of these wild plants you see everywhere. There was this old lady in the village who was a farmer and to make extra money she would harvest oregano, dry it and sell it to the locals.

SS: One of my favorite Greek facts is that there are over 600 endemic plants here. Do different herbs require different geographies, even within Greece?

EK: Herbs are very local, even in Greece. But many aromatic herbs are quite sturdy and will grow wherever you put them, unless you try to do something extreme—you can't plant a mountain herb next to the sea, for example, but you can take oregano from Greece and put it on your balcony in France. What changes is the flavor profile, because the flavor is directly connected to the terroir. You can drink a sauvignon blanc from two different regions—the variety of grape is the same, but it's not the same wine. And that's quite similar to herbs. Oregano gets a lot from the surrounding nature and this helps build the flavor profile. When we are talking about an endemic plant or a local variety you have to think that this herb or plant has developed a character over years and years and it's not something you can replicate. It happens with tomatoes—everyone complains that Northern European tomatoes taste like nothing. People come to Greece and think everything tastes amazing, but the food here is simple and not sophisticated. We are just cooking with quality ingredients.

SS: Does this impact regional styles of cooking around Greece?

EK: Yes and no. Of course, the ingredients that we source are used in many places in local recipes, like island oregano with lamb. But it's not limiting in that way. I lived in Italy for many years, and learned a lot from Italians. Good pasta is something you find everywhere. I wanted our herbs to be like that. When you are cooking pasta you don't think you are cooking Italian, you think you are cooking a staple ingredient. I want our herbs to be thought of as a staple ingredient.

SS: There's a Masanobu Fukuoka quote I love, about how we must eat herbs along with the seasons to encourage a gentle spirit.

EK: There is a huge culture around wild greens which are harvested and put in pies, or boiled and turned into a salad. Around Easter, when they are still tender, it's a very good time for wild greens. Foreigners just think of spinach, but in villages, every old woman knows at least 10 wild greens growing nearby. My mother knows how to harvest the greens from the wild when she is making a pie. This is a big part of our culture, like fresh fennel in spring. They put the fronds in pie, in the Peloponnese or in Crete. These are ingredients that are really local because they're not the subject of commercial transactions, and people just harvest them. In a city like Athens, the best-case scenario is there's someone at the farmers market selling them. I bought poppy weed and wild asparagus last weekend to make an omelet, but these are things you'll find twice a year.

SS: I think that, at least in the West, herbs are often just thought of as food. Is that the case in Greece?

EK: For centuries, herbs were the main source of medication for people. Every family would have tinctures and essential oils for different ailments. But honestly, the biggest and most important use in Greece is the culinary aspect. In Crete, for example, they have tales about dittany, which is a beautiful, fuzzy, very fragrant plant. They call it *erondas* in the local dialect—which comes from *eros*, meaning love—because it grows in steep places where it is difficult to harvest, so they think someone has to be truly in love to find and harvest dittany.

SS: So many people spend the time and money to buy top-quality cheese, meat or organic vegetables, but they buy supermarket herbs. Why are herbs treated differently?

EK: It's partly a supply chain thing. The herbs that we find in the supermarket are cracked into tiny pieces because it's easier to package them. But think about good coffee: It has a short lifespan. You buy fresh coffee, it's delicious, and two weeks later it tastes different! I think the reason people are not familiar with the concept of quality herbs is because they haven't had the opportunity to taste them. I see the expression on people's faces when they taste our herbs—you don't have to be an expert to appreciate food, it's physical.

SS: There are a lot of rules around harvesting herbs in Greece, and a lot of pushback against that. What do you think about the regulations?

EK: You have parts of Greece where certain plants are almost extinct from overharvesting. The level of damage people can do from overharvesting and harvesting out of season is huge. If you take part in it, you can't know the consequences that it may have! Everything has its role in the ecosystem. So I'm pro regulating harvesting. The old lady that we talked about at the beginning of the interview, who would harvest a bit of oregano, was just one person. She didn't harvest much and that was okay, but the world is different today.

(FRANCE)

A HOME IN ARLES.

THE MEDITERRANEAN

François Halard
built his reputation on
photographing other
people's homes. Now, he's
turned the lens on
his own interior.
Words DAPHNÉE DENIS
Photos FRANÇOIS HALARD

Though it isn't his primary residence, renowned interiors photographer François Halard considers his home in Arles his "primary folly." When he first laid eyes on the *hôtel particulier* some 30 years ago, it was love at first sight. The grandeur and Mediterranean cachet of the 18th-century house, in the center of France's "most Roman city," reminded him of the celebrated Italian home of the abstract expressionist Cy Twombly. In a poetic turn of events, the beauty of Halard's home in Arles would eventually be the thing that convinced Twombly to open his doors to Halard's lens.

"When I went to see him, he didn't want to be photographed at home," Halard recalls. "I said that it didn't matter, that I just wanted to meet him because his art was the first I'd acquired, and that I'd bought my house because it looked like photos of his. He asked to see it, and after looking at pictures, he said, 'Listen, you have two days to do as you please.' People understand better what I want to say when they see my home in situ."

A testament to Twombly's lasting influence, the entrance to Halard's Arles home is now an altar of sorts dedicated to the artist. "I was fascinated by how he found inspiration in things that were 2,000 years old, and managed to turn them into something that was radical and modern," the photographer muses. Arles, a former Roman provincial

capital famous for its amphitheater, was also an inspiration, he adds: "For me, civilization was born around the Mediterranean Basin. That idea makes me dream. It was fundamental in the project around this house."

Halard has spent his life capturing intimate details inside the homes of artists like Twombly, Louise Bourgeois and Robert Rauschenberg, offering a peek into the soul of their owners. Yet, until recently, he'd spent little time photographing his own place. Usually based in New York, he and his wife found themselves spending longer than usual in Arles when the world shut down during the coronavirus pandemic. A *New York Times* assignment to portray his confinement, and a conversation with his friend, curator and publisher Oscar Humphries, convinced him to turn his lens on himself. Unable to access labs to develop analog film (he doesn't work with digital cameras), Halard decided to use Polaroids to rediscover his home through photography.[1] "It was a way to look at the light moving across the rooms, to have time to go from one place to the other," he explains. "For work, I'm always running back and forth, and so this was a way for me to learn to take the time to look at the things surrounding me."

Unlike working on commission, this project allowed him the freedom of choosing his own constraints, but the process itself felt no different than photographing the home of another artist, says Halard: "The camera creates a distance between you and your subject, even when it comes to your own interiors. What I'm interested in is to reflect not only the sensitivity of the film itself, but also my own sensibility when it comes to my history and the objects I'm photographing."

Each room tells a different story, with objects and artifacts acquired over a lifetime of travel. Halard places them with care, creating a conversation of sorts between his belongings—African masks, sculptures, photographs, books that no longer fit his bookshelves, all exposed as if in a museum. On the mantel of the master bedroom's

fireplace, two photographs of Picasso's hand, captured by Brassaï, sit next to each other, one a postcard acquired years ago, the other a large print, which Halard found later on. "I like the idea of fragments," he explains. "Of owning a collection of fragments. It can be a Khmer head, a wood engraving by Hokusai which my wife gifted me, mixed with a human fist in marble. Like broken pieces of humanity."

Over 30 years, the three-story house has slowly blossomed into what Halard considers a "family home that I invented." At first, he recalls, he only renovated the kitchen and the bathroom, keeping a camp bed in the middle of a room being demolished, with no other pieces of furniture around. Renovations continue to this day: "I just finished fixing the windows; some of them hadn't been changed since Louis XV, or the French Revolution, so they were... somewhat damaged," he says. Time filled in the empty spaces with memories and meaning. Now, the house itself feels like it may have become Halard's confidante, he says: "You share memories with family members, you trust them. That's how I feel about my house, as if it were alive."

(1) The images that appear over the following pages are unpublished photographs from Halard's *56 Days in Arles* project—vignettes of his home and day-to-day observations made during the COVID-19 lockdown.

(left)   Cy Twombly's *Roman Notes* and a Piranesi lithograph hang in the entrance of Halard's home.

(right)
Twombly's Italian home in Gaeta is
Halard's great inspiration. Like Twombly, Halard
has classical antiquities—Grecian amphoras
and Roman busts—on casual display.

"I like the idea of owning
a collection of fragments... Like broken
pieces of humanity."

(left)   Halard has spent 30 years renovating and arranging the rooms of his Provençal home to his taste.
(above)   Halard's mastery of composition extends from his photography work into the material assemblages that grace his mantelpieces, shelves and desks.

(left)
Halard's 18th-century home comprises
some 22 rooms, including a library, print room,
two archive rooms and a painting studio.

THE MEDITERRANEAN

Photography: Emma Trim

The artist Yto Barrada on co-founding a cinema for the city that inspires her art.
Words AIDA ALAMI Photos EMMA TRIM & KARIMA MARUAN

A CINEMA IN TANGIER.

Yto Barrada discovered the magical world of film when she moved with her mother to Tangier at the age of seven. As a child, she often went to Cinema Lux, located in the city center, where the projectionist would let her sit on a chair beside him to watch a movie.

Some decades later, Barrada, who is now a successful multimedia visual artist, still enjoys watching films from the projection box.[1] But today, she is doing so in a cinema she revived and saved from the neglect afflicting theaters across Morocco. Located in the old part of Tangier, a city on the tip of the African continent, Cinémathèque de Tanger is an art space that is unique in Morocco. Not just a movie theater, but also an art gallery and café, it sits on the city's famed 9 Avril 1947 Square, also called the Grand Socco.

About 15 years ago, Barrada managed to corral a collective effort to help her buy the old and crumbling Cinema Rif and turn it into the iconic venue it is today. "Just like the cafés in Hamra in Beirut, if you don't put your hands on them quickly, they start disappearing," she says, speaking over Zoom from New York, where she lives part of the year with her husband and two children. "That's what happened here. Things were being transformed with neon, new modern air-conditioned buildings. It was a very difficult project to put together because we got very little support. But it also made so much sense in Tangier." In general, Barrada is opposed to the city's rapid gentrification. "I can't stand that they're manicuring the gardens. It drives me physically crazy. They put in too many streetlights," she laments.

Since it opened in 2006, Cinémathèque de Tanger, now a nonprofit, has become the epicenter of culture in the city. The theater, built in the 1930s, has been progressively renovated. Not long ago, viewers were still given blankets during cold winters; now the

coffee shop attracts tourists, locals, young and old.

Barrada was born into a family of activists and intellectuals. Her father is the Moroccan journalist Hamid Barrada, who was sentenced to death in the 1960s for his political activism, and went into exile for many years before his exoneration. Living in Tangier after her early childhood in France, she has always been aware of her privilege, and worried that opening an art cinema in Tangier would contribute to inequality in the city. To combat this, she made sure to make the theater a welcoming place. With a full slate of easy-access cultural events—including special screenings for children—it is also a place where artists are encouraged to meet, to be inspired and to create and exchange.

While renovating, the architect patched the old granite floors and found vintage decorations at the nearby Casabarata flea market, creating a strong visual identity in blue, yellow and red. An old-school marquee at the entrance still displays the names of the films that are showing. The monthly programs, which open like a newspaper, are designed over stills from iconic films like *Hiroshima Mon Amour*, *All About Eve* or *My Sweet Pepper Land*. Many people take them home and frame them. It is also one of the last theaters in Morocco—if not the last—to show films on reel-to-reel.

Barrada has left the day-to-day running of the cinema to others, but she is still a part of it. And sitting in the café remains one of her favorite activities. As a photographer, she spent years walking through the city that has inspired so many writers

"I think the bad rep made it special."

and artists, discovering its backstreets and getting to know its people. Tangier itself and multiple rich experiences have defined much of her artistic career. "I think the bad rep made it special," she says. "It's a port town. Here, people have strong survival skills. It was economically abandoned for years. The consequence to all of that was that it became a space of freedom."

Tangier isn't a city that reveals its charms easily. So many people pass through it on their way to Europe, not taking the time to discover its secrets and adventures. "You have to deserve it. That's the trick," Barrada says. "Nowhere else in the world am I as happy as when I wear my boots and walk in the mud in the rain, or eat a *kalinté* [chickpea flour pie] on the street. There is nowhere else I feel at home."

(1)   Barrada's work is deeply tied to Morocco and to the history of the Mediterranean. Her exhibition at Pace Gallery in East Hampton earlier this year, for example, featured a selection of textile collages dyed using natural sources from her garden in Tangier; paper collages responding to the 1960 earthquake in Agadir; and furniture sculptures that used traditional Moroccan wicker weaving techniques.

Right & Overleaf Photographs: Karima Maruan

الأفلام اليوم

FILMS DU JOUR

التذاكر

BILLETTERIE

TARIFS CINÉMA

DEMANDEZ VOTRE
CARTE DE FIDÉLITÉ
GRATUITE

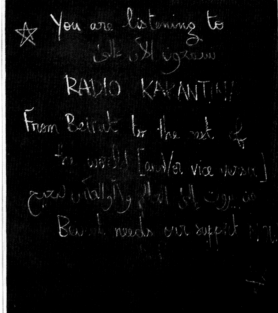

☆ You are listening to
راديو الكرنتينا
RADIO KARANTINA
From Beirut to the rest of
the world [and/or vice versa]
حيث تروي المآسي والأحلام
Beirut needs our support

The cinema was renovated by Atelier d'Architecture Lalo and includes a 300-seat theater and a second, more intimate 50-seat room.
Vintage posters and furniture help to bring the building's late 1930s Art Deco style inside.

CINEMA RIF

سينما الريف

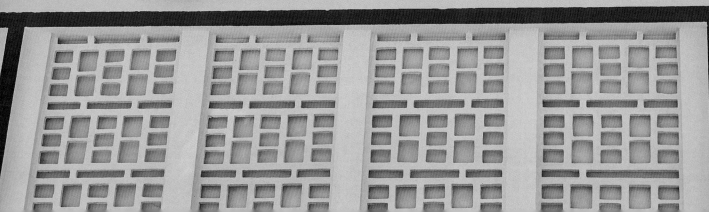

Curator ALYA AL-MULLA shares the legacy of Algerian artist Baya Mahieddine.

In Baya Mahieddine's works, the woman is always the focal point. There aren't any male figures in her paintings. There are some works where you have a female with an infant. But then again, that's an extension of the woman herself.

Baya was born in 1931 and orphaned when she was around five or six years old. She was then raised by her grandmother. Later on, she was adopted by the French intellectual Marguerite Camina Benhoura. It was after seeing Baya drawing and painting in the mud, and making clay figures while her grandmother was working in the garden, that Benhoura adopted her and nurtured that talent. Benhoura had a huge impact on Baya's life. She was a painter herself, and she had a big collection of works in her house which was frequented by many collectors and people in the art world. So that female presence—her mother, her grandmother and her adoptive mother—had a huge influence on her.

Baya's works are extremely playful: very colorful and vivid, very childlike and joyful. She said in an interview that when she paints, that's her happy place. That's where she goes to escape. She lived through the Algerian War and the struggle for independence, but none of that sadness shows in her works.

While curating the exhibition, we didn't want to present her from a Western point of view.[1] When people talk about Baya Mahieddine, it's mostly through the viewpoint of her solo exhibition in Paris which was held at Galerie Maeght. The narrative would normally be that she was this exotic female artist from Algeria who exhibited in France and was discovered by André Breton and Picasso. We tried to move away from that and present her from an Arab art history perspective. So we didn't want to add any extra text panels and contextualize the individual works: You have the introduction, then you walk into the rooms. It's up to the visitor how they perceive what they're looking at. We have some quotes from artists and people who encountered her, and one of them is from Breton. But it's not the main focus of the exhibition. The other quotes are from Arab art historians, other points of view. We respected her as an artist who didn't want to be categorized.
As told to Baya Simons

(1) Earlier this year, Al-Mulla and Suheyla Takesh co-curated an exhibition on Baya Mahieddine at the Sharjah Art Museum in the United Arab Emirates. Al-Mulla's favorite work in the show is *Musiciennes* from 1975, which shows women playing musical instruments. "Baya was very much inspired by her surroundings, and in 1953 she got married to a musician. After that, we notice she started to include musical instruments in her works. It's a happy and cheerful painting with a lot of vibrance and, once you go into that room, you can visualize the surroundings and feel the ambience. You can almost hear the music," says Al-Mulla.

OBJECT MATTERS

Words:
John Ovans

The strange, hermitic history of
the garden gnome.

"The hermit is never to leave the place, or hold conversation with anyone for seven years during which he is neither to wash himself or cleanse himself in any way whatever, but is to let his hair and nails both on hands and feet, grow as long as nature will permit them."

Not to be confused with your personal care routine during lockdown, the above quotation comes from classical archaeologist Sir William Gell's book *A Tour in the Lakes Made in 1797*, in which he outlines one of the most curious professions in history—that of the ornamental hermit.

Once the height of fashion, the hermit was an individual—usually an agricultural worker—hired by a rich landowner to live in a purpose-built hermitage on the grounds of their estate. The job description often required them to dress like a druid, not speak to anyone and neglect their personal hygiene to further the bucolic aesthetics of Georgian England.

In the Romantic era, the presence of such a person was meant to remind visitors of the worthy search for spiritual enlightenment. Having a hermit lurking in the gardens would, in theory, make the landowner seem more intellectual by association. Recruitment was difficult, and there is a recorded case of one hermit who was sighted at the local pub, beer in hand, just three weeks into his tenure.[1]

The craze for ornamental hermits was a fleeting blip, but the notion of the "garden helper" never quite went away—particularly in Britain, where the upper classes have always walked a fine line between tacky and tasteful. In 1847, Sir Charles Isham brought 21 terra-cotta figurines, or *gnomenfiguren*, back from Germany and dotted them about his rock garden. Today we know them as garden gnomes, who are generally bearded, bedecked in a pointy hat and possibly smoking a pipe or holding a lantern.

In the years since Isham first introduced this invasive species, gnomes have come to be considered far from aristocratic; eventually they were deemed so vulgar that they were banned from London's Chelsea Flower Show. Many decried the ban as anti-gnomist bigotry. In 2015, about a hundred gold-sprayed gnomes picketed for equal rights outside the show's entrance.

Gnome lovers faced a distressing shortage during the pandemic due to supply chain disruption and the Suez Canal blockage. Since we were all inadvertently living as wild-haired recluses anyway, perhaps there was no need for them after all.

---

(1) The life of a hermit still appeals to some, however. In 2017, Stan Vanuytrecht was hired to take up an unpaid residency in a 350-year-old Austrian cliff-side hermitage. Over 50 other people applied for the posting.

CULT ROOMS

Words:
Stephanie d'Arc Taylor

Inside ALEXANDER CALDER's studio, where chaos and kinetic art found a harmonious balance.

Photograph: Evans/Three Lions/Getty Images

The work of Alexander Calder is kinetic, fluid, constantly in motion. He's best known for his elegant mobiles (the term itself has its origins with Calder; Marcel Duchamp applied it to his work after visiting the sculptor's studio). These are abstract, colorful shapes cut from sheet metal, which hang on wires and are perfectly counterbalanced with either more sheet metal or a weighted ball. His mobiles, as well as much of his jewelry, painting, and other work, are just-so abstractions—gossamer delicacies which gently respond to changes in their environments like chiffon-wearing dancers. "Each element [is] able to move, to stir, to oscillate, to come and go in its relationships with other elements in the universe," Calder wrote in 1932.

The exquisite precision of Calder's work stands in stark contrast to the state of the atelier where he based his practice for most of his career. The repurposed icehouse—which stood adjacent to the farm in Roxbury, Connecticut where he lived for 30 years—was an utter shambles; Marie Kondo's living nightmare. Pliers, hammers and scissors of all sizes lay on worktables in orgiastic metal jumbles interwoven with bits of string too short to use. Pieces of discarded wood and metal from generation upon generation of project were swept under the table and left there. The mess was illuminated in brilliant detail by nearly 20 feet of soaring windows. Mobiles hovered from the ceiling as if Harry Potter himself had suspended them in space.

The fluid motion of Calder's work, as well as the apparent chaos of his atelier, seem understandable when considering the artist's upbringing and life before relocating to rural New England. Born in 1898 to artist parents—a four-year-old Calder posed for a sculpture by his father, a cast of which is part of the permanent collection at New York's Metropolitan Museum—Calder and his family moved from Philadelphia to Arizona, to Pasadena, to New York and to San Francisco all before he turned 14. He then shuttled back and forth between New York and California for high school, completed college in New Jersey and got a job as a mechanic on a passenger ship sailing from New York to Seattle via the Panama Canal.

While he was working as a timekeeper at a lumberyard in Aberdeen, Washington, Calder felt called to become an artist. He moved back to New York, and then to Paris.

It was in Paris that Calder, like so many of his peers in the heady days of Paris' *années folles*, came into his own. Awestruck by the abstract, geometrical paintings of Piet Mondrian, whose studio he visited in 1930, Calder began exploring geometrical shapes and primary colors in his own work. Ultimately, he infused his abstractions with life by animating them: hanging them from the ceiling and letting them sway freely, or even powering them with a small motor. One of the latter pieces, *A Universe* (1934), was particularly captivating to Albert Einstein, who allegedly stared at it for a full 40 minutes when it was first exhibited at New York's Museum of Modern Art.

But like for many other expats enjoying the moveable feast that was interbellum Paris, the energy of the scene proved exhausting after a while. Calder and his wife, Louisa (née James, the grand-niece of the author Henry James), moved to Connecticut in 1933 after courting and marrying in Paris. His life until then had been exciting and dramatic, with new stimuli coming in at rapid fire. In Connecticut, that changed: Calder settled in, raised two daughters with Louisa and developed his artistic practice at the Roxbury farm for the next three decades. Life was simpler (although he and Louisa did manage a three-month trip to India in 1955, where he produced nine sculptures as well as some pieces of jewelry). But the chaos on which he so obviously thrived lived on in his madhouse of an atelier.

It was at the beginning of the Connecticut years that Calder began to be recognized as one of the foremost sculptors of his generation. He also started to amplify his mobiles to monumental size, creating large-scale installations he called stabiles. These were instantly popular; Calder was ultimately commissioned to produce stabiles to be displayed at New York's Idlewild Airport (now JFK), UNESCO's Paris office and at the 1968 Mexico City Olympics.

But as the years passed, the old wanderlust returned. Calder left Connecticut in 1963, decamping for Europe once again.[1] The second Atelier Calder was outside Tours, France. There, scraps and bits didn't have decades to accumulate. But from the photographs we have, it seems that by the time he died in 1976, the piles were well on their way to Roxbury levels.

(1) Calder's legacy lives on in Roxbury, Connecticut. His 1975 sheet metal sculpture *Angulaire* stands on the grounds of the Minor Memorial Library, the city's public library, on South Street.

MIKE LEIGH

Photograph: Rick McGinnis

The remarkable director discusses starting from nothing, over and over again.

The British director Mike Leigh has been making critically acclaimed films and plays for 50 years. He is perhaps best known for his collaborative, improvisation-led approach, which involves rehearsing with an ensemble cast over an extended period of time. Much like real life, a Mike Leigh film is recalled not in chronological plot terms, but in single, impressionistic shots that contain everything there is to know: a mother standing in the doorway of her teenage daughter's bedroom in *Life Is Sweet*, the way Vera Drake holds her cup of tea, or the listless quiet of a London street in *Naked*.

POPPY BEALE-COLLINS: Where are you speaking to me from?

MIKE LEIGH: I live in London, but I'm based in Cornwall in this moment. I've been isolating here for over a year. I miss my kids, and my grandson, and all that stuff, but we're connected by [online] means. We were supposed to make a film last year, but I don't think I can realistically do anything under COVID conditions until probably next year, given the way I work.

PBC: Does the way you work, under normal conditions, involve much writing?

ML: The writing process is part of the process of working with actors and building up the whole world. I actually don't write anything, in that conventional way. I'll have ideas on the go. *Secrets & Lies* and *Vera Drake* came from specific notions: *Secrets & Lies* out of the fact that people close to me had

adopted, and *Vera Drake* from the fact that I'm old enough to remember what it was like before the Abortion Act. But even then, making those films was very much a journey of creating the characters and investigating the relationships over a long period, and building scenes through rehearsal. Writing is through rehearsal. The writing is very precise at the end, but it's not arrived at by my going away and writing a script and bringing it back. The vast majority of what we wind up with comes out of improvisation. All the 20-odd films I've done have come out of [this] process.

PBC: Has all this downtime meant that you've done more reading?

ML: Yes. There's never enough time to read everything you ought to have read. And given what I quite often am doing, my tally is even worse than it ought to be. About 18 months ago, I was having a conversation with somebody and Philip Roth came up, and I realized I'd only ever read *Portnoy's Complaint*. I've now read everything Philip Roth ever wrote. You get into habits. People say, "What are your influences?" I always say, and I truly am, influenced by Yasujiro Ozu. Then I suddenly thought, I've got quite a comprehensive collection of his films on Criterion box sets, but haven't watched all of them. There's a certain level of hypocrisy about that. So I sat down and watched all of Ozu.

PBC: Until the last year, you'd spent most of your working life in London. How important

is location to your creative process?

ML: I am a people-watcher. I get actors to talk about people they know and that stimulates or resonates with ideas I may or may not have. There's less people-watching in Cornwall, but that's not really an issue. I'm not sitting here thinking, *Oh my God, I'm not seeing people and I'm drying up*. After over a year of it, I am, slightly inevitably, suffering from [the feeling of] *Have I wasted this last year? Why didn't I write a novel?*, but it depends on what you call wasting your time. My natural habitat has always been theater and filmmaking, because it is about collaborating. It's about the craic of the team, and the fun of that really. That's part of the stimulus.

When we make these films or plays—and I'm very uncompromising about this—we get an empty building, like a school, so it's a complete space, a laboratory to really explore in an uninhibited way. The working environments, the disciplines are really important. Also, speaking as one of the greatest procrastinators in history, the great thing about how I work is that I have to get up and be there at 9 o'clock every day for six months, and that's nonnegotiable. I've got to go and make something happen, and some days are more creative than others. And that for me is one of the "secrets of success"—the fact that you've got to get in there and do it. Get involved. You can't phone it in.

BAD IDEA:
STEREO TYPE

Words:
Debika Ray

The omnipresent embarrassment of "exotic" type.

Vincent Connare, the creator of Comic Sans, has long defended what is widely considered the world's worst font. People who dismiss the childish font "don't know anything about design," he told *Dezeen* in 2014.

There has been no such vocal defense of so called "ethnic typefaces," those which appropriate the aesthetic flourishes of foreign scripts to suggest that a brand has exotic origins. Yet they continue to be part of the visual noise of Western countries, screaming out from food labels, restaurant menus and posters. To anyone familiar with the alphabet being aped, they are about as authentic as the British tourist who wishes his companions *bone apple tea* prior to eating.

So-called "chop suey" fonts, which mimic the brushstrokes of Chinese handwritten characters, have been around in the US since the 19th century—as much an American invention as the food it is named after. On Indian products, you'll see typefaces that

Photograph: Stephanie Gonot

fecklessly incorporate the horizontal connecting line used in Devanagari text, while Middle Eastern connections are often suggested using fantastical imitations of Arabic calligraphy. In some instances, letters are substituted with ones that look similar—the Greek sigma (Σ) and omega (Ω) instead of "E" and "O," for example. This confusing practice becomes more egregious when the letters bear no phonetic similarity, such as the Cyrillic Я (pronounced "ya") and И (pronounced "I") for R and N.

It's clear why these fonts become popular, even adopted by ethnic groups themselves as an easy way of marketing businesses to foreign audiences, but it's also obvious why they're increasingly shunned. The use of cultural stereotypes, often in combination with lazily conceived imagery, feels uncomfortable, especially given the lack of ethnic diversity in the graphic design and advertising establishments.

The use of such fonts have long inculcated a narrow and small-minded view of non-Western cultures. "All type and design is subliminal, no matter how monotonous or garish," said designer Tré Seals, in a 2019 interview. He set up Vocal Type, a foundry that strives to "introduce a non-stereotypical piece of minority culture into graphic design, taking inspiration from protest signs at such events as the American civil rights marches, anti–Vietnam War protests, battles for women's suffrage and Stonewall riots."[1] His goal is to contribute to a graphic environment that "cares about telling the stories of the people we serve and not the false history of the industry we work in."

(1) Seals is currently working on a typeface inspired by the infographics of W.E.B. Du Bois. Du Bois' data visualisations were designed for the 1900 Paris Exposition to commemorate the lives of African Americans at the turn of the century, and to expose the structural forces of oppression that were denying African American progress.

GOOD IDEA: DIFFERENT STROKES

Words: Harriet Fitch Little

The awareness that fonts are not neutral, but come loaded with their own history and cultural reference points, is spurring designers to diversify the offerings available. Graphic designers on the African subcontinent (where the Latin alphabet is used de facto in many countries) have taken up this challenge with particular urgency. In 2014, the Zimbabwe-born graphic designer Osmond Tshuma created a typeface called Colonial Bastard Rhodes, created using type elements from racist advertising published during the British imperialist era. His typeface was explicitly made to draw attention to how loaded seemingly neutral lettering can be. As he later explained in an interview: "Colonialism was an act of brutality clothed in the farce of civilization." Other typefaces created in recent years attempt to replace the cartoonish "tribal" style of so-called African fonts with something more nuanced. The Kenyan graphic artist Kevin Karanja created Charvet in 2013, a typeface born of his love of ancient African typography and geometric shapes. Meanwhile, the iconic typeface of popular restaurant franchise Nando's, which serves African-Portuguese food, was redone in 2016 by the sign writer and artist Marks Salimu, who painted the characters directly onto wooden panels. As a representative from the chain wrote at the time: "It not only tells the story of who we are and where we've come from, but importantly, it puts our people at its heart."

ISLAND HOPPING

Crossword: Mark Halpin

ACROSS

1. Big tubs in a winery
5. "To err is human," and the like
11. Blue Grotto locale
12. They might be seen in the company of dalmatians
14. Smartly dressed
15. Made like new again
17. Mediterranean island that's in a grumpy mood?
19. Life story, in brief
20. Emergency life-saving technique
21. Where to do some island-hopping
22. Ruffly decoration
24. Just the tiniest drink
26. Messy substance from a Mediterranean island?
30. Iraq's main port city
32. Entices with bait
33. Drink one orders regularly on a Mediterranean island?
38. Use as a chair
39. Beauty whose face "launched a thousand ships"
41. Newspapers and TV on a Mediterranean island?
46. Return mailer, for short
47. Ancient theater or old cinema
48. Regret
50. London-to-Madrid dir.
51. Edge of a cup or crater
52. Mediterranean island that is very likely to exist?

CORRECTION

Words:
Harry Harris

The messy reality behind a simple prescription.

The Mediterranean diet is often touted as a sort of anti-diet: a recipe for health and longevity that revolves around the region's celebrated love of olive oil, vegetables, nuts, seafood and the occasional glass of red wine.

But even this seemingly less dogmatic prescription is laced with complexity. First, the evidence is questionable: Much of the credit applied to the Mediterranean diet was fortified by a 2013 study run by PREDIMED, which has now been widely discredited, since approximately 20% of the participants were not randomly selected.

More importantly, it is hard to say what the Mediterranean diet actually refers to. Eating habits differ wildly between Tunisia, Israel and Albania, all of which number among the 22 countries that hug the sea.

Greece, Italy and Spain are the countries most associated with the Mediterranean diet in the popular imagination, but even here there is division. In Italy, for example, the reliance on olive oil varies region to region, with northern Italy traditionally favoring lard as a cooking fat. More generally, it seems that all countries—including these lands known for fresh rosemary, sun-ripened tomatoes and plump figs—are now eating more processed foods, meat and saturated fat. As far back as 2008, *The New York Times* published a piece of handwringing under the headline "Fast Food Hits Mediterranean; a Diet Succumbs."[1]

The problem when looking to prescriptive diets of any stripe is that they all fight with each other. Keto diets are low carb, high fat. The Harcombe Diet instructs you to avoid candida. "Clean" diets demonize sugar and processed foods. More importantly, they also don't work in the long term, with a 2020 study from the *British Medical Journal* concluding that the desired effects of most diets largely disappear after a year.

To the extent that the Mediterranean diet offers a better alternative, it is because of its flexibility: It is a broad set of guidelines, rather than a rigid prescription. But dining out on a sliver of salmon and a Greek salad doesn't truly capture the health and happiness of eating freshly caught fish by the sea in Athens. The biggest problem with focusing on the potential health benefits of any diet is that they often ignore the more immediate benefits that come from eating: the joy of tapas, antipasti, bowls of olives and plates of dolma. If longer lives are associated with countries in the Mediterranean that follow these principles of joyful, sociable eating, maybe the love they have for their food is a part of that. Perhaps that's what we should be striving for.

(1) The Food and Agriculture Organization of the United Nations published a report in 2008 that signalled the Mediterranean diet had "become just a notion." In reality, the report stated, the region's diet had "decayed into a moribund state."

Photograph: Lauren Bamford. Food Styling: Stephanie Stamatis

LAST NIGHT

Words:
Bella Gladman

Photograph: Ezra Patchett

What did creative director PEPI DE BOISSIEU do with her evening?

Pepi de Boissieu is based in Barcelona, but you're equally likely to find her in France, Senegal or the Spanish countryside. Born in New York, but having grown up in Argentina, the peripatetic art director has made a career out of her flair for creating a convivial atmosphere. Whether in her creative installations for the likes of Hermès, or her new holistic home project, Dora Daar (run in partnership with her best friend, Nat Sly), she combines exquisite food, thoughtful workshops and beautiful visuals to create experiences and spaces to remember.

BELLA GLADMAN: What did you do last night?

PEPI DE BOISSIEU: A bunch of friends popped in without notice, and we had a few beers together on the terrace. I live alone but I have a very open house.

BG: How do you prepare for unexpected guests?

PDB: It happens quite often! I go to the local markets every couple of days so I usually have a supply of fresh delicacies. Last night it was artisanal cheese, hummus, anchovies, bread and butter, and vegetables with olive oil. I've recently started producing my own olive oil, as there are olive trees by my place in the country.

BG: So you're often found in the kitchen?

PDB: I love to cook for myself, as well as for friends. I have a friend with whom I exchange recipes and hers always include instructions like: "While you caramelize the onions, you need to sip a little bit of wine." It's essential. I also like to listen to Brazilian music like bossa nova while I'm at the stove.

BG: Did you stay up late last night?

PDB: I'm not a late-night person. I much prefer the daytime. So after my friends went home, I had a wonderful bath with essential oils and went to bed with a book. I'm currently reading a graphic novel—not my usual choice, but I'm really enjoying it.

BG: Do you have an evening ritual?

PDB: An older lady I knew in Paris had a routine that I liked so much I do it too. Every night, I follow the same route around my house to light all the lamps progressively, flowing with the light that they give, starting from little candles, through to a soft lamp and onward.

THE GREEN RAY

Words:
George Upton

A flash of inspiration.

In the final scene of Eric Rohmer's movie *Le Rayon Vert*, a young woman sits with a man she's just met, watching the sun set over the sea. Just as it disappears below the horizon there's a brief but unmistakable flash of green—the last fleeting moment of sunlight. The green ray, after which the movie takes its title, is said to offer a flash of clarity into one's feelings and those of others.

Scientifically, the green ray can be explained by the way light is refracted and separated by the earth's atmosphere as the sun approaches the horizon. The often-elusive phenomenon—people can spend their whole lives looking for it—took on a semimythical significance when it was first popularized by the publication of Jules Verne's *Le Rayon Vert* in 1882, a century before Rohmer's movie was released.

Verne's characters travel to Scotland in search of "the true green of hope." Rohmer's own quest for the green ray led him to the Canary Islands. While certain atmospheric conditions do need to be present, the American Association for the Advancement of Science advises that the green ray can be seen anywhere that offers an unobstructed view of the horizon—often that means the sea, although apparently the top of the Empire State Building does just as well.

Whether you find that the green ray does indeed inspire a sudden moment of clarity will depend on if you're ever lucky enough to see it.

STOCKISTS:
A — Z

A	APRÈS SKI	aprèsski.es
	ARDUSSE	ardusse.com
B	BON VENT	bonvent.cat
	BOTTEGA VENETA	bottegaveneta.com
D	DRIES VAN NOTEN	driesvannoten.com
E	EDWARD CUMING	edwardcuming.com
F	FRITZ HANSEN	fritzhansen.com
G	GOOSEBERRY	gooseberryintimates.com
H	HEREU	hereustudio.com
	HERMÈS	hermès.com
	HOUSE OF FINN JUHL	finnjuhl.com
	HUGUET	huguetmallorca.com
I	IAGO OTERO	@iagootero_
K	KENZO	kenzo.com
L	LRNCE	lrnce.com
M	MARSET	marset.com
O	OMEGA	omegawatches.com
	ORIOR	oriorfurniture.com
R	RICK OWENS	rickowens.com
S	STRING	stringfurniture.com
	SYNDICAL CHAMBER	@syndicalchamber
T	TINA FREY	tinafreydesigns.com
V	VERSACE	versace.com

MY FAVORITE THING

Words:
Diébédo Francis Kéré

Architect DIÉBÉDO FRANCIS KÉRÉ, interviewed on page 86, explains the significance of his carved stool.

This small wooden stool, carved from one piece of wood and decorated with intricate carvings, holds the quintessence of my childhood. Known as a *gho* in the Bissa language, which literally translates to "sitting wood," it represents comfort and a sense of being held close and cared for. This is because whenever I saw my mother sitting on it, I knew she was either about to start preparing a meal or some other activity that was connected to family life. These stools would get carried from one corner to the next to allow people to perch next to a stove to stir a stew, or next to some bowls to shell peas or to gather together and talk.

When I see these stools today or trace my finger along their carvings, I am transported back to Gando and, more importantly, to those memories that anchored me within my community and family and which to this day nurture my work. I seized the opportunity of designing my first pieces of furniture to pay homage to it. And so, the ZIBA came to be. Both the original stool and the ZIBA mark an important period in my life and it delights me that, through a design process, I could connect seemingly transient moments: my childhood of carefree play and arriving at a place in my work as an adult when I was free to design as I wanted.